House of Pain-The Rayner Sisters' Story

By

Jeanette Williams

ISBN: 1-4033-0552-8 (Electronic)
ISBN: 1-4033-0553-6 (Softcover)

This book is printed on acid free paper.

1stBooks - rev. 05/20/02

ACKNOWLEDGMENTS

My deepest gratitude goes out to all my friends and family who supported me throughout the writing of this book.

Walter Williams, my husband, for his support and encouragement and patience, which kept me motivated to keep on going with my dream, and to my two children, Clarissa and Walter Jr.

To Elaine, Yvette, Inez, and Teresa, my sisters, who have given me a lot of help in putting this novel together.

To my parents, who have instilled in me the knowledge that I can do anything in the world if I just put my mind to it.

A special thank you to the Lord above, for I would not be here to write this book had he decided not to wake me up everyday.

To Angela and David Hernton, Gail, and Glida, and Mr. and Mrs. Theodore Mills, my spiritual family, for their understanding and devotion, as well as their constant cheering me on to finish what I had set out to do. They truly are a blessing from heaven, and will always be in my heart.

And a special thank you goes out to all the foster parents of the world who have given up everything to devote their lives to taking care of children who are need of a home because of abuse and neglect, and giving those children the chance they deserve to become whatever they reach for in life.

WILLIAMS/HOUSE OF PAIN

The story begins with three little girls, who had a hard time growing up in 1965. They were always treated badly, beat constantly, and never allowed to do the things other girls did. Their life was filled with constant schoolwork and scrubbing the floors in the house. Jollena and her sisters were expected to do their homework and still do the mopping and waxing of the living room floor. One day, while they were in school, the children services came to their home to take them away from their parents. The father didn't understand why this was happening to his girls and the mother just sat still and didn't move an inch. They were told that someone reported the girls had been mistreated. This news was the first that the father had heard about the girls being abused by their mother.

Their life was never easy for them as children. They had started to except what would happen to them the next time their mother got mad. So, when the news came to them that they were going to be taken away from the only home they had ever known, they cried at first, then things started to come together for them. They wouldn't have to be beaten or punished again for things that were not their fault. Tanya, who was the oldest of the three, had to try and explain to the other two that nothing was going to happen to them. She was the inspiration for both Ivana and Jollena when they thought that going to a home would mean being locked up for the rest of their youth.

When asked if they would be together in the same foster home, Tanya told them that they would. She didn't want them to be upset anymore. She didn't tell them that they might be separated from each other. She also didn't tell them that it was a good chance that they all could be put in a situation where they needed all the help in the world to deal with this sudden situation, that was thrust upon them. The day came for all three girls to leave for the foster home that was chosen, as the place where they would be living until farther notice. "I don't want to stay here, said Ivana, with tears starting to row down her face.

Tanya looked at her sister, with such emotion, she too started to cry. "I know you don't want to be here but, if you go back home, things will still be the way they were before we were taken away. Do you really want to go back, Ivana? Do you like being beat on all the time for something that wasn't your fault?" The girls stood together and just hugged each other till the counselor came from the back office to talk to them. She stood at 6ft and looked like a warden from a women's prison. She had the look of sternness on her face as though she were glad to be putting the girls away from their family. Her name was Miss. Downfield and she had no children of her own. There were rumors that she could never get a date because men were afraid to approach her, so she never got married. That's probably the reason why she looked the way she did. She stood there looking at the three black children with a very stern expression on her face. "My name is Miss Downfield, and I'm here to talk to you three about what is going to happen to you all." She moved to a chair near the girls, so that she had a better look at who she was to deal with.

"Who is the oldest of the three of you?" She waited for an answer, with her hands folded on her lap.

"I am the oldest," said Tanya.

"Okay, I guess you are the one I can get the answers from. She pulled out a notepad, and an ink pen from the pocket of her blue dress.

"Now, tell me what has been going on in your home, Tanya". How has your parents treated you girls?

Tanya was starting to get scared because she knew that she would have to tell this woman all the things she and her sisters had gone through, while their dad was at work or someplace else other than home. She knew she would have to tell how her mother had abused them because, she blamed them for being born and destroying her marriage. She once told the girls that if she had not had any children at all, her and her husband would be close again.

"Tanya, I'm waiting for your answer". Is this going to be too difficult for you to talk about?"

"No Madame, I can do it but, I don't know what to say first".

"Just say what's on your mind". Miss Downfield looked at her as though she was a mute child who couldn't give a right answer if her life depended on it.

Tanya decided to tell her only a little of what she wanted to hear. My mother used to beat us because she thought that we were doing things wrong around the house. We were placed in the corner, on our knees for a long time, until we heard our dad come in the door. Then she would make us go in the basement to play or do some schoolwork, to keep us from telling our dad what she did.

"Tanya, how old are you?"

"I'm 10 years old, Madame. Jollena is nine and Ivana is seven".

"Tanya, can you tell me a little bit about what your mother used to beat you girls with? Do you have any marks or bruises on any part of your body?"

This was starting to get a little easier for Tanya to talk about so, she started her story the best way she could. She wanted to make sure that she didn't leave out anything that might be important to this lady. This was going to be the factor in their going home or going somewhere that was safe for them. It was up to her to get the facts right and not to leave out anything that was important, She may have been only 10 but, she had a lot of sense when it came to her and the younger girls' future.

The girls had a lot of talking to do with Miss Downfield in order to get things out in the open about what they had gone through in that big house, while their dad had no clue or just wished not to accept what he saw or heard, when he was at home. Everyone that Miss Downfield talked to told her the same thing about the girls being beaten with extension cords and sticks. She was told by some of the concerned neighbors about how they saw bruises on the girls in places like their backs and thighs. Some of the cuts had pieces of copper embedded in them to a point where they had to be removed with tweezers.

The family also told about how the girls were made to kneel in the corner, with their hands up in the air, until their mother told them to get up from the floor. A lot of the time, they weren't lucky enough to get up off their knees but, to put their hands down only. The only time Tanya and the girls were able to have fun was when the mother decided to go out with her friends. They would sneak in the kitchen and eat bread with sugar (they were called sugar sandwiches), and raw oatmeal. When the mother found out what they were doing, she beat them with the extension cord while their bodies were wet.

The school told Miss Downfield about how the girls would come to school with bruises on their legs and arms that looked like someone cut them with a knife. They were so bad that, the girls were too embarrassed to take gym because, they would have to take off their clothes in front of the other girls who, after seeing the bruises, would either make fun of them, or just stare at the marks in shock. These beatings were done so much that, the girls started to except them as part of their lives.

For a while, things were going kind of good for the battered girls. Their cuts healed and they were happier. Their grades rose up a lot, and Tanya was even on the track team in her school. Jollena still wasn't up to the point where she wanted to take up any kind of sport. She preferred to sit by herself and read a book, or work on her poems that she was so fond of doing. It kept her mind off things that she was trying hard to forget. This was a way for her to release all her thoughts and to heal the best way she knows how. Ivana spent a lot of time with her friends and got into a lot of trouble at school as far as fighting is concerned. She thought that violence was the answer to all her problems that she was having. It was the only way she could heal.

They were getting on with their lives and no one was going to interfere with how they wanted to live. After a while, Tanya started doing little things that were not in her best interest to be doing. She was not doing her homework and the teachers were constantly on her about skipping classes. These were things that she, as a young girl, were not suppose to be doing. She became interested in boys and men. Her dresses and skirts became shorter than they were suppose to be, and her friends became the important thing in her life. Throughout this hold thing, the foster parents didn't know what to do with her. They were at their wits end and needed to talk to Tanya's counselor about placing her in another foster home.

This isn't what the guardians wanted for the girls because, they had always been together and now it was all over for them. Tanya was going away to live with another family, and the other two were scared that they were next on the list. Mr. and Mrs. Greenwich had done everything they could to keep the girls together and they really didn't want to let Tanya go because, they knew she had potential to be anything she wanted to be, if she could just put her mind to it.

Three months later, Ivana was placed in the home of Miss Alice Thomas, a hard- core, very unpleasant woman who, even though she excepted another mouth to feed, didn't really want another girl in her home with her real children. She had never married but, had a boyfriend who had been very abusive toward her when she was 20 years old. He drank a lot and smoked 3 packs of cigarettes a day. It was 1949 and there was not a lot of good jobs around for black males. But, Sam Porter had a good job working at the steelyard five days a week, for $1.50 an hour.

Everyday was hard for Alice because, she had to finish school and go to work for a nice white couple in the valley. There wasn't much for her to do but clean, cook, and watch the couples' two young children. She had no other skills that would take her away from this kind of job so, she continued to do this work until she was let go because the couple was moving to Santa Barbara, Ca.

Alice eventually got a job working in an office building, doing the same kind work she was accustomed to doing, working as a cleaning woman. She met Sam while she was out on the town one New Years Eve, with two of her co-workers. She thought he was a good-looking man with his tall, slender body, muscles of an weightlifter, and long slick- downed hair. He was 22 years old and she was 19. They met that night and agreed from then on, to continue seeing each other on a regular bases.

Things were good as long as Sam didn't drink too much. He could be a very gentle man to be around and to get married to. Alice eventually moved in with him because, he had a big house downtown, on Central Ave, in ST.Louis, Mo. This was the area where all the blacks, who could afford it, moved to where they wanted to raise their children. This was an area where all the houses on the block were lined with rows of flowers that smelled of a beautiful fragrance.

"Oh Sam, this is the most beautiful place".

"Yes, and it's all for you, Alice". You can do whatever you want to with the rooms, as far as decorating is concerned, said Sam, smiling his most.

"I love it here". Alice stood in the big bay window that's in the living room. He had taken care of this house. It gave her the pleasure of opening the front door and letting the warm summer wind come through. She walked in the kitchen, looked it over from the big stove, to the modern refrigerator sitting in the corner of the kitchen.

"Yes, she would do whatever she wanted with this house. She would take care of it the same way that Sam has done.

"Could you recommend a good woman for a very lonely man?"

Alice turned toward Sam and ran into his arms. This was the man she wanted to spend the rest of her life with. She looked into his big brown eyes and kissed him fully on the lips. Sam returned the kiss more passionately then she had done. He held her close to his body and ran his hand down her back. He wanted her more than anything he could ever drink. He stopped kissing her and looked into her eyes for what seemed an eternally.

"Will you promise to stay with me for as long as we both can stand each other?"

"I will", Alice said with the most honest, sexual look she could give.

With that, Sam pulled her closer to him and kissed her even more than he had done before. He kissed her all over her neck, ears, and shoulders. Alice could do nothing but let him take control of her and do to her whatever he pleased. But, just when she thought that her

8

legs would give out from under her, Sam stopped kissing her and said that he would be back later.

"Where are you going, Sam? said Alice, with a look of puzzlement on her face.

"Look, I won't be gone long". And he stormed out the door, got in the car, and drove away. Alice stood there in the front door, staring into space wondering what she had done to make him want to leave in such a hurry. Was this the beginning of something she didn't want to take part in? Or was she just jumping to conclusions about Sam?

Six hours later, Sam returned home, drunk and loudly talking to himself as he stumbled up the front steps. He didn't look like the same man that had left her hours ago. This was someone else Alice didn't even recognize as being her man. His clothes were hanging off him, and his hair resembled a mangled wig. Alice stood there staring at this man she didn't even know. She wanted to run to him but, something told her not to go near him while he was in the state that he was.

"Alice, come here and give your man a big hug." Sam yelled, as he fell up the last step.

"No Sam, you're too drunk".

"What do you mean I'm too drunk?' It ain't nothing wrong with me gal, so come and do what I said.

"Sam, you're embarrassing me in front of everybody in the neighborhood". Please come in the house.

9

"You can't tell me what to do, woman". At the last word, Sam fell backwards down the steps and hit the back of his head like an egg breaking on the sidewalk.

"Oh my Lord, Sam". Alice screamed, as she ran out of the screen door and down the steps. At the same time, others in the neighborhood started to gather around Sam's house, to see if they could help in any way they could. Two men picked Sam up and took him into the house, and laid him on the sofa. Blood had begun to run out of the gash in the back of his head. There was a 2-inch opening at the base of his skull.

"Will someone please call the ambulance", said a big, heavy-set woman from down the street. She was the kind of person who would take care of everyone.

"Sam, can you hear me?" The woman kept calling him, till she decided to take his pulse and respiration. From watching all this, Alice could tell that the woman knew him really well. Who was she and how did she know who he was? Alice tried to keep from crying out loud but somehow it came out. She screamed so loud that everyone in the living room turned to see what was going on. She tried to scream again but nothing came out this time. Her mouth was wide open but there was no sound. Alice couldn't catch her breath, then fell to the floor. The woman who had been working on Sam turned toward Alice, bent over to roll her over on her side, and gave her a couple of slaps on the back. Alice suddenly let out a scream, which could be heard from three houses down the street. The woman held her for a few more moments before going back to Sam, who was unconscious on the couch. Another woman came into the house and asked if she could be of any help. She ran into the kitchen to get a pan of water and a towel. They both managed to control the bleeding until the ambulance arrived. Alice was looked after by the two women, while the emergency crew worked on Sam. The trip to the hospital wasn't an easy ride for Alice. She didn't say a word when the ambulance pulled into the hospital.

"Don't worry Mame", said the EMT. He will be alright in the hospital. They will take good care of him for you, so don't worry about anything.

"Will I be able to talk to him?" Alice asked, with a rather shaking voice.

"Yes, as soon as the Dr. says you can, the nurse will come and get you". Then the EMT shook her hand, then left with his partner.

This was the worst three hours Alice had ever had to wait before she could see Sam. No one came to let her know what was going on with him. She walked back and forth trying to calm herself down so she wouldn't be a nervous wreck when they did come to get her. She had only known this man for a while, and she loved him. No matter what, she was going to stick by him through this tragic time of his life. She needed him, and he definitely needed to have her around in order to keep him happy.

"Miss Thomas, you can see him now", said the nurse, who had come into the waiting room without Alice knowing she was there.

"Will he be alright after the blow he received to his head?"

"I 'll let the Doctor tell you what to expect from his recovery", the nurse said, as she adjusted the IV tubing in Sam's arm. Soon, the Doctor appeared in the room.

"Hello, Miss Thomas, how are you feeling?" My name is Dr. Tolts.

"How is he doing, Dr. Tolts?"

Dr. Tolts took off his glasses and said, "He'll be just fine as soon as he is able to talk again".

"What do you mean by that, Dr.Tolts?" Alice looked at the Dr. as though he had just cut her heart out.

"Well, he has a compound fracture of the skull, which protrudes a little bit against his brain. But, it's not as bad as it seems. His brain sustained a little damage to the nerves, which controls speech".

"Can this be corrected?'

"Yes, with surgery and physical therapy, he will be back to his old self again".

"When will he get the surgery?' Alice needed to know everything, so that she could be able to cope with Sam being sick for a while.

"We have scheduled it for tomorrow morning, at 8:00a.m."

Alice thanked the Doctor for his time, and then sat down in a chair, in the room where Sam was being watched by the nurses on duty. Why did he have to go and get drunk like he did? Why don't he just give up drinking all together? These were the questions that kept going around in her head, as she sat watching her man lay in a hospital bed with tubes in his nose and IV in his arm. It had to stop here and Alice was going to try hard to make him understand that if he kept on living this way, he was not going to be so lucky next time.

The next day, Alice got up early so that she could be at the hospital just in case they needed her. She took a shower and tried to eat something but, for some strange reason, she was starting to get really dizzy. She shrugged it off and headed to the hospital. She had only been there for 15 minutes when she started feeling very sick again. She had been so busy with what was going on with Sam that she totally forgot about her own health problems. She had gone to see Dr. Wiltsman two days before all this took place. He had told her not to get stressed out anymore and get some rest. She was so glad to be with Sam that, she forgot to tell him that she was going to have a child.

Sam was in the recovery room by the time Alice got back to the hospital. She asked the nurse how he was doing and went into the room to sit next to his bed. She kissed his cheek softly. "Oh, Sam I love you so much," she whispered.

She held his hand tight. Again the dizzy feeling came over her, "Oh, Sam! Oh, Sam!" she repeated to herself in almost unendurable agony. "What a hell of a father you are." She sat there for what seemed to be an eternity, watching this man who had almost ended his own life by drinking. How was she going to tell him that they were going to have a child, and they hadn't talked about marriage yet. He took her virginity away from her and never once said he wanted to marry her.

Just then, Sam opened his eyes and looked around to see where he was. His mouth moved, but he couldn't say the words he wanted to speak. Alice had to tell him everything that happened to him for the last eight hours. All the time she was explaining his condition to him, she could feel tears starting to fill her eyes. After she was through telling him of his condition, she reached for his hand but he just pulled away from her. He looked at her once more before turning away. Alice knew then that this was not going to be easy. She came to the conclusion that he just didn't want to have anything to do with her at this point.

Two months had gone by and things were still bad between Alice and Sam but, she was not going to give up on him because, after all, they were going to have a baby. She had not told him that she was pregnant. She thought it would be better if she waited till he was better before she sprang this news on him. Sooner or later though, he was going to have to know. On the way home from the doctor's office, Sam and Alice didn't say a word. The window was open in the car, and hot, wet wind caressed her face, blowing through her hair, arousing her senses. She felt an overwhelming need for some sort of a conversation. She glanced at Sam, watching his handsome, strong profile. His face was so expressionless, which scared her.

"Sam?" She broke the silence.

"What is it, Alice?"

"I want to talk to you about something, if you don't mind".

"Not right now, Alice. Can it wait till we get home?" He gave her a faint look before turning back to the road. His voice sounded a lot better then it did two months ago. he was making a remarkable recovery.

When they arrived home, Sam parked the car, handed Alice some paperwork out of the glove compartment, and headed toward the house. Alice removed herself from the car and walked up the sidewalk toward the house. Once inside, Sam turned and looked at Alice with such patience, that she was afraid to look at him. He wanted to talk to her but, couldn't bring himself to say anything to her. She has had enough of this silence and starts to walk into the living room where he was sitting on the couch. "Sam, I have to talk to you about something very important. You have to listen to what I have to say this time, okay?"

"Alice, if you're going to preach to me about my drinking, I'm not in the mood for it".

"No Sam, it has nothing to do with that at all. This concerns the both of us." Alice gets up from where she was sitting, and sat next to Sam.

"What's wrong?" Sam asked.

Not wanting to wait any longer, she told him that she was going to have a baby, and that she was three months long. Having to finally get this off her chest, she could sit back and wait for him to answer.

"Why didn't you tell me this when you found out yourself. Why did you wait so long to bring out this information?" It would have been a lot of help to me to know that you were carrying my child.

"I was going to tell you on the day of the accident but, you left before I could get out a word about it. Then, when you returned home, I still didn't have the chance because, you had gotten drunk.

"Alice, I'm so sorry. I didn't mean to put you through anything that would jeopardize the life of our child".

He got to his feet and knelt in front of Alice. His hands slid over her shoulders, and she put her arms around his neck. It had been a long time since they last held each other close. Sam, shining from the lamp on the end table, tall, lean, his black, straight hair around his face, seemed almost too beautiful to be alive.

He let his hand flow thru her hair, then run down her cheeks, stopping to outline her lips with both index fingers. His touch continued down her neck to her breasts. He wondered what she would look like in a couple more months. His warm, strong hands caressed her belly and moved slowly down her body. She felt such a need to be crushed in his arms. He took her in his arms, She could feel his heart beating. Then he dropped his arms, pushed her away, and sat back down on the sofa.

"Just look at you, Alice", he said. "You are more beautiful then I had imagined. You're covered all over with that smooth, brown, satin skin, and your eyes are as black pearls. Your hair smells of perfume. You could have met anyone you wanted to while I was in the hospital, but you didn't. He sat there just staring at her with such apathy.

"How could you even think of such a thing, when you know that I love you more than anything on this earth?" Who would be better

16

than you?" Besides, I'm going to have your child, not some other man's, but only yours.

Alice was twenty-two. She could only see her future, a future as Sam's wife. It's what she always wanted. Sam had to know that she cared a lot for him. He had to know that no matter what happened, she was going to stay by his side. She only hoped that he would be willing to meet her half way.

Six months later, little Nashina was born. She was the perfect little girl for both proud parents. Sam had been the perfect father by getting everything ready for the baby's arrival. He had no parents to tell the news to, and neither did Alice because, both their parents were dead. They both had no other living relatives. They were alone to enjoy this occasion by themselves. For six months, Sam didn't have the desire to get anything to drink. Alice knew in her heart that this was going to be great for the both of them. But, things didn't last like Alice had hoped. The baby was now nine months old, and Sam was beginning to go back to his old habits again of drinking heavily. Sometimes, he wouldn't come home after work but would go with his buddies instead, to the liquor store.

This was the final straw for Alice because, she had warned him about his habits and threatened to leave him if he didn't stop what he was doing and come home, where he was supposed to be. This particular day, Alice felt that something was going to happen but, she didn't want to think about it because, she had a lot of work to do around the house, before he did get home. She heard the car pull up and kept doing what she was doing in the kitchen. Sam came in the house, staggering as usual. He found Alice in the kitchen and started to fondle her. She rejected his advances by pushing his hands away from her body.

"Why did you pull my hand away, woman?" He stood in front of her, looking down at her and breathing alcohol in her face. She turned her head away from him to get a breath of fresh air.

"I'm not in the mood for your nonsense today, Sam".

"Well, I'm in the mood for you, babe". Now, come and sit on my face and let me have my dessert. I mean, come and sit on my lap and let me have my food". Alice couldn't stand to be next to him so, in a last result to get away from him, Alice pushed him really hard, out of her face. If she was never sorry before, this was the day that she would be very sorry that she had laid a hand on a very drunk, silly man. He took one look at her and started to beat her with the skillet that was sitting on the table in the kitchen. Alice tried to get away from him but he was much too strong for her. She had never seen him this way before, and it scared the hell out of her.

"Sam, please stop". Don't hit me anymore.

"I'm going to make you pay for this, you slut. I'm going to make sure you know who is master in this house".

Alice was then thrown to the floor and beaten half to death with his fists. He had no mercy on her at all, and she was too weak to do anything to defend herself from this monster who, beat her senselessly, then tore off all her clothes and raped her. He penetrated her so hard that, she began to scream from the pain that he was inflicting on her. The floor was covered in blood from her ordeal.

She managed to let out one more scream that startled the neighbors who could hear. Someone called the police, and two officers broke into the front door. They ran into the kitchen and stood in disbelief, at a crazed man raping a badly bruised, blood-soaked woman. They drew their guns, and ordered Sam to get away from Alice, so that they could try to save her life. The ambulance arrived shortly after the police, and they worked on Alice for what seemed to be hours, trying to stop the bleeding from many wounds that she had on her.

Six weeks later, Sam was sentenced to 25 years in jail for the attempted murder of Alice. He tried to call several times, to talk to her but she refused to have anything to do with him. The house was hers now because, it was part of the lawsuit that she filed against him, which was for pain and suffering she received from him. She was offered the chance to tell her story on a television station but she declined the offer, because she just wanted to sell the house and move somewhere else with her daughter. Her life had to start all over again but she didn't care.

Years passed before Alice would even think about starting a new relationship with anyone else. She wanted to be with another man but she was afraid to trust anyone with her heart again. She had gotten herself a new house, another job, and her daughter was now a teenager.

"Momma you need to get out more because, you're not getting any younger, you know".

"Nashina, I'll be okay. I don't need to be going out looking for no man at my age".

"But, you sit in the house too much. You only leave here when you're going to work. You need to get out and enjoy yourself".

"I'll be just fine, thank you very much. If I need some company, I'll call Miss Henser to come over for awhile. She loves the idea of coming over so she can see what I bought for the house".

"Okay, momma, you win. I guess you know what's best. Well, I got a date with Antonio. I'll be home by eleven, okay?

"Okay but, make sure you don't go over this boy's house with him. You make him bring you back here. If he doesn't want to follow the rules, then you call me and I'll come pick you up"

"I'll be just fine momma. I know what to do". With that, she ran out the front door and got into Antonio's car. A loud, butt-end up, down in the front, black thing out of some ghost movie. Surprisingly enough, the car was named "Gray Ghost".

Time passed and Alice finally found someone to share her life with her. He was an accountant on the same job with her but on a different floor. His name was Paul knicks, a successful, black man, in his mid- forties. He was a tall, muscular, well-built man, who Alice fell in love with only after he kept trying to make a date with her. She finally excepted his invitation to go out to dinner. They dated for almost two years, then she found out that she was again pregnant. The relationship lasted until he was sent to prison for embezzlement. Now, nine months later, she gave birth to a set of twins that she named Nelson and Nick. She vowed never to see another man again. She had her three children, and that was all she needed until she was talked into becoming a foster parent.

Ivana didn't like the idea of staying in this house with a woman who seemed to be upset because she had to be a foster parent to a strange child. But, it was either here or go back to her mother. Miss Thomas took the girl's belongings to the room that she would be sleeping in until farther notice.

Ivana walked around the house trying to get familiar with everything in this lady's home. She wanted to see how this woman lived and how many children she had of her own. With success, she found out about the boys and an older sister, who was away at college in Nebraska. The boys were at school. They went to a private school, that was paid for by their father, who had managed to save up quite a lump sum, before going to prison. The rest of the money came from a trust fund that Mr. Knicks had never used, which belonged to him. He turned half of these funds over to Alice, to use for the boys.

The first day went by kind of good for everyone in the house. Ivana spent a lot of her time doing her daily reading of her favorite books called "Little house on the prairie". She basically related to Nellie, and wished that she could be more like Laurel Engels. But, that wasn't about to happen any time soon for her. She got the chance to meet the boys when they got home from school. Miss Thomas had told them a little bit about Ivana coming to live with them for a while.

"What school did you go to at the time of the sentencing?" Nick smiled to her when she came into the kitchen that evening.

"Where did you get the idea that there was a sentencing?" She looked at him like he had just told her she was not wanted.

21

"I didn't mean anything by it, I was just trying to make conversation with you, that's all".

Ivana couldn't do anything but smile because, she had never heard that saying before.

She was beginning to loosen up a little more. Maybe, just maybe, there was hope for her yet. What did she have to lose.

"So, what do you little Turks do when you're not at school?" She looked at them with a smile on her face. She could tell that they were very smart boys so, she should have guessed on her own that they do a lot of studying.

"We do a lot of things when we're at home." Why do you want to know so much about us?" asked Nick, with a look of disapproval on his face. He was starting to not like the way she was so busy trying to find out so much information about them.

"Oh, never mind what I just asked you two." Ivana realized that she had invaded their territory, and she understood what it was like to have someone prying into business that didn't concern that person. She never asked them anything else because, then she would have to tell everything about herself and her sisters, which she had no intention of talking about at all, to anyone.

Miss Thomas came into the kitchen just after Ivana spoke those last words to the boys. She didn't look too good today and there was signs that she was ill. But, she had always been a strong woman, who could take a lot of pain and still bounce back into framework with whatever it was that she was doing. So, she started to clean up the kitchen while the kids ate their snacks. She kept an eye on Ivana because she wanted to make sure that she was not a threat to her boys. At the same time, She could see a lot of herself in this girl. She knew what it met to be living in someone else's house and not your own. She had, at one time, been in the same situation when her parents were killed in a car accident. She knew that she would have to help Ivana in every way she could, without getting too close.

"Ivana, I want you to make sure you unpack all your belongings before you go to bed tonight." She turned to look into Ivana's direction.

"I already took care of all my clothes, Miss Thomas. I put them all away when I first came here. She looked as if she was looking for approval from this woman.

"Mama, can we go outside and play for a while?" asked Nick, with the look of anticipation.

"Yes, and please try to stay in front of the house, so that I don't have to wonder where you both are."

With that, the boys took off running to go and play with the kids next door. Ivana was left sitting at the kitchen table all by herself, with nothing to do but stare at MissThomas cook. She was a good cook and could beat anyone at the stove when it came to whipping up a special meal. She had learned how to cook from Sam. At least that was something she could remember about him that didn't scare the dickens out of her.

After dinner, Ivana did the dishes and cleaned the floor before going to bed. It wasn't right for her to be locked up in the house so much. She didn't have any friends to talk to because Miss Thomas didn't think it would be a good idea. But, things would be much better for her the next day because, she was going to school. Ivana was in the 4th grade and was an A student. She adjusted with no problem at all. She made a lot of friends and adjusted to not being able to see her other sisters. Maybe one day they would get back together again and things would be the same.

While everything was working out for the girls in one respect, all was not well in the home where Tanya was staying. She started off on the right foot but then, things began to drop for her. She got into trouble with the law and had to spend some time in juvenile detention. She made the mistake of hanging out with the wrong crowd of people and it caused her to start stealing anything that she thought she could get away with. Her and the weird bunch would walk into a department store and pretend to buy something while the rest of the crew grabbed anything they wanted from off the shelf. and racks of clothes. She even went so far as to participate in a robbery of a drugstore, where she was one of the ones who carried a gun.

After this escapade of trouble, she went back into the juvenile detention center for another sixteen months until she turned 18, where she would be placed in an institution for women. While there she escaped and was hard to find again. No one had an idea where she went. The law couldn't catch up to her because she was busy moving from state- to- state. During this time, she managed to move into another home with another family in Ohio. The law did catch up with her later on, and she was taken back to the detention center. When the girls found out about this, they thought their sister had just abandoned them. They were left to take care of themselves after they were able to be released from the children's services.

During this time, Jollena was living with an elderly couple who treated her like she was their own daughter. They never once yelled at her or hit her for any reason at all. She seemed to enjoy staying there with this couple. They had never had any children of their own so, getting Jollena was the best thing that could have happen to all of them. Jollena was in school as soon as the couple found out that they were going to get her for a while. She adjusted to this life as if she'd been there all alone. This was where she wanted to stay for the rest of her life.

Jollena was fine for a while, until she started feeling lonely during the holidays so, she decided to ask Mr. and Mrs. Fieldman when her sisters could come to live with them. She hoped that they would understand what she was going through and decide to help find a way to get them there.

"Mr. fieldman, do you know how to get in touch with my other sisters?" She waited for an answer. Can you talk to someone about bringing them to me, even if it's only for a short time?"

"I'll see what I can come up with. I have a few friends at social services, who I can get to look and see what they can get on your sisters. But, I can't promise you anything on this, though. So, don't get your hopes up too high about finding them" He took her hands and held them for a long time before telling her goodnight.

By noon the next day, it was all over. Mr.Fieldman came into the kitchen holding a piece of paper in his hand. "I'm sorry Jollena, but they couldn't find anything on your sisters. It seems they were separated some time ago. Their whereabouts has been kept so much of a secret that, the workers are not able to pinpoint where they have been taken. Jollena didn't say one word for the rest of the day. She just stayed in her room and stared at the walls, thinking about the times they shared together while they were still living at home. This was the hardest thing she had ever had to deal with. But she knew that one day she would see them again.

Eventually, the whole affair faded away into the background. Jollena forgot all about trying to find her siblings and got on with her own life. She found herself getting involved with other girls in the neighborhood, who were her age. Her grades began to improve a lot more and she joined a couple of clubs at her school. Just when she had started to get herself together, another tragedy took over. Mr. Fieldman went to the hospital because he was feeling rather badly. But, it was more than that because, in reality, he was suffering from pneumonia, and there wasn't much of a chance for him. It was merely a question of hours.

Mrs Fieldman had been contacted by an undertaker whom she had known for a long time. This wide-awake man gained an advantage over his competitors in that he went after the business while the others waited for the business to come to them. This enterprising fellow called on Mrs. Fieldman early the next morning.

"Mrs Fieldman," he said surreptitiously referring to the slip of paper he held in his hand with her address and name on it. "I sympathize with you in your grief. I give you a thought: What has come to you has to come to all of us."

Mrs Fieldman understood. "When the time comes, how much would you charge for a simple funeral?

"Now don't you worry about costs," he said. I'll give him a fine funeral. There's no man I respect more than Mr.Fieldman. I'll make it my personal business to see that he gets the best there is. Don't worry about the money."

When Mrs. Fieldman returned to the hospital the next day, a doctor asked her to come to his office because, he had some bad news for her. But, she already knew what it was about. Mr. Fieldman had passed away during the early morning. When she got to the office door, she saw Paster Kotts there. He had come to help with the arrangements that had to be made. The doctor asked necessary questions, like the full name and place of birth and so on. Three days later, the funeral services took place, and Mrs. Fieldman and Jollena said their good-byes.

As time went on, Jollena was to get the biggest surprise of her life. She was going to move with one of her other sisters, at the same house. This was the day that she had been waiting for. This was the moment that she had hoped would come true. This was going to be a reunion. Mrs. Fieldman was not going to be her foster parent anymore because, she was moving to San Antonio, TX, with her sister. She sold the house that she and her husband lived in for what seems like an eternity. These two had to start their lives all over again and they were looking forward to it.

The social worker arrived to take Jollena to the home she was to stay at next. She hated to leave Mrs. Fieldman by herself but, she told Jollena that she (Mrs. Fieldman) was leaving that same day for the airport. Jollena said goodbye and left with the social worker.

"Will me and my sister be together from now on?" She grinned and waited for an answer from the woman. She wanted to make sure that they would not be separated again, that is why she kept wanting to know all the details of the case.

Yes, you will be able to stay with your sister until the state decides what to do with you girls." This should be a wonderful time for you both, now that you'll be together again, don't you think so?"

"I can't wait to see her. We have a lot of making up to do. There are a lot of things we have to talk about." This was truly going to be a wonderful day for Jollena and her sister. This was like a dream that she did not want to wake up from. Now her life was complete again.

The car pulled up to the gray and white house that sat on the corner of the street. It was an old Victorian house that stood three stories high and, there was a white picket fence around the front of the home. The yard was well taken care of and there were plenty of flowers to look at and smell. An oak tree stood in middle of the yard with a bench around it for sitting on under the shade. There was also a bird house perched in the tree, with it's bright colors of red and white glimmering from the sun shining on it. Jollena stood at the car, too afraid to move because she didn't want to lose the moment that she was having. But, she decided to make her way up to the house and stand in front of the door, waiting on her sister to come out and greet her with hugs and kisses.

The moment of truth had come for them to meet, after many months of being apart from each other for so long. The door opened, and this girl with long braids stood in front of the screen door, watching these two people standing on the porch. It was Ivana. They both reached out and grabbed each other and refused to let go The woman who drove her there, stepped into the house to talk to the foster parent who would be in charge of the girls. Her name was Miss Alice Thomas.

The girls stayed with Miss Thomas for 6 months before they were told that they will be going home to their parents again. They didn't like this idea too much but what could they do? They had to do what the caseworker told them to do when it came to being moved around. So, they had to pack up their clothes for the move to the place they had left behind so long ago. What would happen to them after they returned home? What would their mother do to them, when she got mad again? These are the questions that needed to be addressed before going back to the arms of their parents.

Mrs. Downfield reassured them that things would be different once they returned to the custody of their parents. She let them know that both mom and dad had undergone counseling before they could get the girls back. This was good news to both Ivana and Jollena, since they are the ones who would have to deal with their mother again. But, before they went home, the counselor had to get Tanya out of the trouble she got herself into. The caseworker managed to plea bargain for her by telling the court that the reason Tanya got into trouble in the first place was because, she had come from an abusive home and had been placed in several foster homes before one would except an older child. She also told the court that it had been difficult for Tanya to adjust to the new home because, she had been torn away from her sisters who, she was really close to. All the girls had been treated badly and the caseworker felt that some of the problem were the fault of the parents.

After a long debate, the judge agreed to let the girl go free, in the custody of the caseworker. Tanya was relieved to know that she was not going to spend anymore time in the court system. She made a vow to herself to stay out of trouble from now on. She would go back to school and stay away from teens that were a bad influence on her. She wanted no more trouble from the guys that she hung out with. Now, the girls were together again and, getting ready to go home to their parents for good. This was not what she had expected to happen but what could she do.

They arrived home around 3:00 that afternoon, accompanied by the caseworker. She sat down with the girls first so that she could explain to them what they had to do to make things better for them and their parents. After her conversation with the girls, she started a meeting with the parents, so that things could be bought out in the open. They talked what seemed like hours before she decided to conclude her meeting with them and leave. Afterwards, the girls went to their rooms in order to unpack their belongings and get ready for dinner. It was weird being back in the same place where things took place. they really didn't want to remember what had happened to them when their mother got mad. But, it was time for them to get on with their life now. Maybe things will be different since they were taken away.

It was in the summer so, there was no school to go to or anyone to talk to because, everyone in the neighborhood was too afraid to talk to the girls. They were scared that the mother would come outside and start something with them. The girls spent the whole summer playing by themselves. This didn't seem to bother them much because, they had each other to talk to.

One day their mother sent them to the store to get some things for dinner and to get themselves something too. On the way to the store, which was across the bridge, they met up with a couple of girls who used to play with them before they had to leave home. For a moment, they just stood there staring at each other, trying to figure out should they speak or keep going as if they had not seen the sisters. One girl by the name Sheila, decided to brake the ice between them and say something to Tanya.

"Hi, Tanya. What have you all been doing since you got back home? Did you like where you were staying?"

"I wouldn't call it being somewhere nice. I had to go through a lot of stuff in order in get along with the people they put me with." She turned away so that they couldn't see her start to cry.

"Are all of you home for good now?" Asked one of the other girls that was with Sheila. They all stood there looking at Tanya, Jollena, and Ivana as though they were looking for an immediate answer to their question. Ivana thought they were being a little bit too nosey. She didn't think that they should be asking all these questions that didn't concern to them at all in the least. "I didn't mean to be asking all these questions, Tanya. We were just trying to make you feel better, now that you all are back home." The girls stood there talking for a little while longer before Tanya thought they had better hurry up and get to the store before their mother started getting mad at them.

The girls made it to the store and back home within 15 minutes tops. If it's one thing they remembered from the past, and that was to never goof off more than you had to because, mother was sure to be watching the clock to see how long it took to get back to the house. But, she was waiting at the door when they got home and she started to yell at them and their dad stopped her in her tracks. She gave them the look as though she were saying, "You won this round, this time but, I will get the chance to talk to all of you about this matter." That look by itself, would make a lion or elephant hurry up and get out of the way.

The summer ended, and it was time for the girls to get up and get ready for school. They really didn't want to go but had no choice in the matter. This was a chance to get away from the house and find some new friends at school. Tanya felt that these so-called friends were no fun to be around with and, she didn't want to have anything to do with them if they were just going to make fun at her and her sisters. This was one bit of aggravation she wanted no part of.

Things were going to change for them one way or another and, she was going to make sure that no kids would talk about her and what her parents did to her, Ivana, and Jollena. Her classes were at a local high school, so she wouldn't see her sisters till they got back home that day. In a way, it was kind of exciting because they would have something to talk about when they did get together. After they finished their chores, they had the opportunity to talk to each other about how things went at their school.

Ivana decided to be the first one to speak about her experiences at Nickles Elementary. She told how she met two nice girls in her class who wanted very much to be friends with her. At first, she didn't want to let them into her world but something they said made her change her mind about them. They told the story about how they found out later in life, that they were adopted by a nice young couple, who had three other kids of their own. At first they, Pam and Michelle Reeds, didn't want to believe that they were adopted. They wanted to see their real parents but the Petersons told them that their parents were killed in a car accident when the girls were only 2-years-old.

They always wondered why they didn't look like either one of the Petersons. They often wondered why the other children at school used to stand in the back of the room, and talk about them as if they were not there. It all became clear to them that they really didn't belong there at all. But, soon it became easier for them to live in a place where there was plenty of love and affection for the two Native American Indians.

Ivana began to cry when she listened to their story about how things used to go in the house between the other kids. These children never wanted them there in the first place because, Indians just wasn't allowed to stay with white Americans. She had never gone through the things that they did but, she understood how the courts could, put a kid somewhere she was not wanted by other children of the family. Tanya declined to say anything about her experience for the day because, even though she was back in high school, she just couldn't make friends like she used to.

A few of her old friends were standing by Tanya's locker that same day when, as soon as they saw her coming, they just turned their heads as though she had mud on her face. Now, these had been the same girls she went to the store with, and talked to constantly during their lunch break.

"Look out girls, here comes the foster home poster girl." Said the tallest girl named Nicky. All the other girls burst into a roar of laughter and giggles, while at the same time, looking at Tanya."

"Yeah, her parents decided to give her up because they didn't want her anymore. Sort of like old clothes and shoes that you don't want anymore," Stated another girl, who used to walk home with Tanya everyday."

Tanya felt like crawling into a hole and cover herself up with the dirt. How could they be so cruel and selfish? What gave them the right to talk about her the way they did? Did they ever wonder to themselves rather or not they could go through as much as she had done? These idiots didn't know anything about her situation at home or in the foster care system.

"You guys need to leave this girl along and go to your classes, and don't ever let me hear that kind of talk again." This was the voice of Mr. Frederick Wells. He was the principle of the high school. He was one to fear if you ever got caught doing something to get in trouble for. Even if you thought about doing something, you can be sure that Mr. Wells knows about it. A retired navy sargent, thirty-third degree mansion, and eighth-degree black belt in Judo, was one to watch out for.

"Young lady, are you alright? Do you want to go to the nurses' office?" If you need to go, come to my office and get a hall pass. Mr. Wells looked at Tanya for a few minutes, then escorted her to his office for the slip of paper. He could tell something was wrong with this child but, did not want to push her into telling him what the problem was. He pulled out a slip of paper from his desk and began to write her a pass.

"What is your name, young lady?" He held the pen still, waiting for her to answer.

"My name is Tanya M. Rayner." She said as she held up her head to look at the principle for the first time. She didn't know this man and was very afraid of him. She thought of him as being one of the ones who put her in foster care in the first place. She really didn't want to tell him her name because, she thought this might turn out to be another person wanting to take away her freedom. "Sir, can I go to my class now? I don't need to go to the nurse office for anything."

"Miss Rayner, I need to know what happened out in the hall to cause three other girls to talk to you the way they did? Did you

35

provoke them in any way or fashion to make them say such things about you and your family?"

Now, here was the last straw for Tanya. She could tell that Mr. Wells wanted to blame her for what happened. She wondered why no one wanted to see things from her side. Why was she being accused of something that was not her fault. From her point of view, she thought the blame should be placed where it belonged. "Mr. Wells, I had nothing to do with how they behaved. They started messing with me because I was in a couple of foster homes." Tanya started to cry and reached into her pocket for a kleenex. tissue. She had not wanted to tell this stranger anything about her family, or anything affiliated with them. She felt as if she had been violated in every way possible.

"Tanya, I know you have been through a lot for the past three years, and I want you to know that, I and a few other staff members are here to help any of our students with whatever problems you, or any of the other students are having. We want you to feel good about yourself here and on the outside. If you need to talk to someone, just let me know and I'll arrange for you to have a meeting with our school counselor. Is that alright with you?"

"Tanya wiped her face, and looked at Mr. Wells for a moment before shaking her head in approval. All she wanted was to be left along to deal with her own situation. Nobody understood what her situation was like, and as far as she was concerned, they never will, no matter how many times she tells her story. Mr. Wells let her leave the office with a note to give to her teachers. She really didn't want to go to class after what she had gone through with the other kids in her school. These are the same girls who played with her and her other sisters. Thank goodness it was time for the bell to ring, so everyone could go home.

Another year had gone by, and the girls were just starting to feel the wrath of their mother again. She seems to have gone out of her way to make the girls' life a living hell. Once, Jollena was still hungry after eating dinner that consisted of small portions of food, that only a two-year-old could get full off of. She asked for some more to eat from her mother who, didn't seem to want to get her any more. Well, Jollena thought she had better ask again, only with a little tears on the side. This little jester made the mother very upset, and all of Jollena's world came tumbling down on her.

Her father came into the dining room and began to argue with the mother. "Why don't you give that girl some more to eat if she wants some?"

"She already had her food." Said the mother, with such hatred in her voice. This fight lasted for some time before he had to leave for his job as a DJ. Two minutes after he drove off in the car, the mother grabbed Jollena and started beating the living daylights out of her. After severe damage was done to Jollena's back and legs, the mother had one more surprise for the girl.

"Since you want to cry about food, I'm going to see to it that you get enough to eat." With that, she went into the kitchen and got the largest cooking spoon she could find. She came back into the dining room and handed the spoon and a large bowl of beans to Jollena.

She then dragged the girl by her long hair and made her stand by the table, and told her to dance like an Indian around the table, while putting the spoon of food to her mouth and repeating the words "UM-UM Good." This humiliation, along with the other sisters laughing at her, only made her want to take the darn spoon and choke herself to death, so that she would be free from the abuse that she suffered, at the hands of the woman who is supposed to protect her. Jollena didn't know too many words, as far as their meaning is concerned but, she had a feeling that humiliation meant, "Those traveling the highway of humility won't be bothered by any heavy traffic." No matter how bad she felt doing this stupid thing, it always came as a shock to find out that her own mother didn't love her.

"Now, take those dishes and put them in the sink. Then, I want you to get your ass in the corner, with your arms in the air." She screamed, as if she were giving orders at a prison farm, even though it felt just like it should be that way, to Jollena.

A couple of hours had passed, and the other girls were in their beds, fast asleep. Jollena was still standing in the corner, with her arms barely holding up. The mother sat on the couch, watching television and reading a book. There was a loud noise outside, as if someone getting out of a car. This was a clue to the mother that her husband was home, and that it was 2:30 a.m. Jollena had stayed in that corner for 8 hours, without sitting or going to the bathroom. The mean warden looked at the helpless girl, and told her to go to bed, and she had better not say anything to her father about what happened, or she was going to be in even more trouble then she can handle. How much more abuse can one kid take from an adult. One can only believe that one day, the girls wouldn't have to take anymore of the harsh punishments their mother had planned for them.

Time passed by quickly for the girls, as they continued to be abused, insulted, and just plain put down a lot. Life with mother had started to get even more severe and sickly. Once their mother accused Jollena of having sex with 6 boys at her school. Now, how on earth could a sixth grader come up with such a nasty, unlady-like, act of stupidity? This was not the thing to do and expect to live on this planet, yet long be able to stand in front of an abusive mother, and tell her that you had done such a thing.

Jollena kept telling her mother that the story was not true but she repeatedly kept at Jollena to tell her the details of the alleged crime. When the girl let out the final word of it didn't happen, the mother beat her with an extension cord, a large belt, and a wooden shoe. The beating lasted for what seemed like hours, before she finally let go of the child because she had gotten tired. This heinous punishment was all that Tanya could take so, she made up her mind that she was going to leave home the first chance she got. She didn't want to leave her sisters but, she felt that things would only get worse if she stayed because, she had thought about killing their mother for the way that she treated them.

Two months later, Tanya split the house that she felt was a prison and, headed for her friend's house. She managed to stay out of sight for a year before she showed up at the girls' school during recess time. She wanted to see how they were doing, as if things had gotten better because she had left home. In reality, things were still the same, with the exception of their dad staying away from home two or three days a week. She gave them some money and said that she would try to see them again one day.

That day never came for the girls because, Tanya was caught trying to stick up a gas station, along with two other men, carrying guns. Tanya had to make a decision about giving herself up or taking the chance and shooting the armed guard. She chose to take a life, in regards to losing her own. This dumb act landed her in "Chitticatta for Girls". This would be her home until she turned twenty-one, where she would be transferred to a state prison.

Tanya was not the kind of person to stay in one place too long so, she decided to run away from the place where she was imprisoned. It was a clever plan she had concocted to get away. She asked if she could work in the kitchen. At first, the guard didn't think it was a good idea but, wanting to trust her, he let her work with some other girls, preparing the morning meal. At the same time, there was a truck delivering goods to the facility that same morning. As soon as he had finished unloading the truck, the driver left the back doors open for a few minutes, while he got a signature from the head cook.

Later that night, there was a search of the institution for drugs that was supposed to have come into the hands of some girls. Upon checking each girl's room, they came upon Tanya's area, and found her not in her bed. A search was conducted but turned up empty-handed. Tanya had gotten away from them and, there was no way they would be able to find her. She had a good lead on them, and they didn't have a clue as to how she got out.

Buy the time two new babies had come into the home, it had been almost three years since the disappearance of Tanya. The girls were getting used to not having their older sister around. This meant that Jollena was now the one responsible for carrying on the older sister tradition, even though she didn't want to be included in this arrangement. Beatings stopped for the time being because their mother was busy caring for the two little girls that had come into their lives. They only hoped that their mother would not be as strict with these two children, as she had been with them. There were four girls in the house now, and the father had his hands full on what to make sure that they had, as far as personal things were concerned. He still didn't stop his routine of staying away from the house more than two nights a week. This was something he felt he had to do, for some stupid reason or another. They kept hoping that he would stop his woman chasing, and stay at home to see what was going on there.

As time passed on, Jollena and Ivana were in high school together, trying to stay out of trouble and staying clear of their mother. Ivana suddenly started back to her routine of fighting in order to get a point across to all bullies who chose to pick a fight with her. Jollena, on the other hand, preferred to stay out of fights because she thought that it only brought out others, who wanted the chance to challenge you. She would let her sister fight her battles for her instead. This didn't always go the way she planned but it was a chance she was willing to take. Besides, Ivana was good at what she did, as long as there was a

41

fair fight. But, some of the time, there were more than one person she had to tackle, which didn't turn out too good for her. She was seriously injured a few times from fighting one girl, while three others hit her in her head.

As things got a little better at home, the mother started going out with her friends on the weekends. This was like a party for the girls because, they had a chance to have fun watching t.v. and sneaking their friend Colleen into the house while their mother was getting dressed. They would hide her in the basement, or on the upstairs balcony. They thought they were getting away with something but some would say that the mother knew Colleen was in the house. She just didn't say anything about it because, she was very fund of the girl, and didn't mind her staying overnight sometimes. One would think this mother was the sweetest person in the neighborhood but, if only they knew how she was when her friends weren't around to keep her mind off beating the girls because their father had been gone all night.

When she started going out more, the husband didn't like the idea that she was starting to look good every weekend. He became very jealous when she left the house. He would come home before her, and hide in the bushes, in front of their house. When her friends dropped her off, he would jump out and grab her by her hair, and start to beat her in front of her friends.

Now, the violence had suddenly turned on her, and she became the person to get beat on all the time. Even when she didn't go anywhere, if he was in a bad mood, he would start to complain about the food, and throw the plate across the floor. The girls were in the middle of something that had frighten them, and now they had to watch in silence as their mother was being done the same way they had to live by, for most of their life.

Once, while the mother was washing dishes, they got into a heated argument about something he had done, and they fought in the kitchen. She managed to pull a knife on him, cutting his arm very deep. He in turn started beating her as if he was fighting in the boxing ring again. Jollena tried to jump in between them and, was hit pretty hard in the face. Ivana ran upstairs and called the police. When they arrived, the father was escorted out of the house, into the police car. They kept him for 22 hours, before releasing him to his brother.

Needless to say, it was two months before the girls were given allowances because, he felt that they didn't deserve to get his money after calling the police on him. So, their mother had to play the part of father when it came to handing out cash. She really didn't want to but, she thought that if she didn't do it, the girls would have to suffer for taking up for her. She decided to get even with him at a later date for having to give up her going out cash.

"When I get the chance, I'm going to beat the hell out of him, while he sleeps." She screamed through the phone, as she was talking to her best friend.

"Ann, don't do anything to make him even more mad at you," said Pam. She was really scared for her friend who had taken a lot from her husband, with his flirting and whoring around.

"Don't worry, Pam, when I get a hold of him, he's going to need a lot of corrective surgery to put things back in place." She laughs at herself, at the thought of disfiguring her husband for life. This way, neither the other woman, or any others he might be messing with, will be able to enjoy him. Let long him having a good time. She sat in the living room for a while, trying to figure out her next move. It would have to be done with great skill and knowledge. her mother once said, "Patience strengthens the spirit, sweetens the revenge, moves anger, subdues pride, and loosens the tongue. She never understood what she meant by that remark but, she knew that her mother had gone through the same things she now faced. She felt that some of the arguments started for no apparent reason. One of the worst spectacles imaginable is the anger of two people who have gotten into an argument over something that neither of them knew anything about. One would say that the greatest remedy for anger is delay. Ann thought that it was never worthwhile to argue about something you never really had in the first place.

Love was always a shortage in the Rayners' family. The girls got their love from the constant beatings they received from their mother, yet got none at all from their father The most lonely place in the world is the human heart when love is absent. The most important thing a father could do for the children is to love their mother. There was only hatred and confusion, along with resentment. The other woman got all the affection he had to give. It's no wonder he didn't have a clue as to what was going on with the children he promised to be there for. Only after the girls were removed from the house, did he realize that something was wrong in his castle. But it was too late to do anything about it, in regards to changing both his and his wife's attitude.

Four years had passed quickly, and the girls got older and wanted to leave home, to go try things out by themselves. Ivana kept leaving, and always came back, but Jollena didn't have the heart to stay. She had weighted her options and decided that when the time was right, she would make her move.

"Ivana, I'm going to leave the first chance I get." She stated, while looking at herself in the mirror, gently combing her hair.

"I thought I would never hear you say that, girl. I was under the impression that you wanted to stay here until you got too old," She laughed as she let those words come out of her mouth.

"It is well overdue, and I need to go while I still have the nerve to get out of here. I want to be able to make it on my own, without having to depend on mama and daddy to take care of me. Even though mama had done a good job of making my years a living hell."

Jollena, I will try to help you get out, if I can," Ivana said, as she gave her sister a hug. Maybe mama will listen to me.

"Yeah, well what if she doesn't see things your way, Ivana? What if she starts to make things worse for you, girl?"

Ivana looked at her sister, trying to find the right words to say to her. "Well, I guess we'll cross that bridge when we get to it, won't we?" She wanted her sister to go out on her own because, she felt that the girl was old enough to handle the world outside of the jail they spent so many years in. She knew Jollena would be just fine and would have a job waiting for her when she gets there. They had planned this action for a long time, and Ivana had the scoop on the ins and outs of where to go.

The day came just two months later when, their mother started an argument with Jollena about her not being her real mother. This made Jollena very mad and, she decided to fight back with a statement her mother didn't expect her to say.

"If you are not my real mother, and daddy isn't my father, then I want to go live with my real parents, today." Jollena didn't know that she could let these words flow from her mouth. She was the quiet one of the girls.

"You will never get the chance to see them because, I'm not going to tell you where they are." This was fun to the mother, and she kept toying with Jollena, just to see her cry and beg to go to the parents she never knew. Even though this was a total lie, she was determined to make Jollena's nerves shoot through the roof.

Jollena had enough of this abuse on her intelligence, and felt that she should tell her mother just how she felt about staying in that house one more day. "Mama, I want to leave here today and go get myself a place of my own. I don't want to live here anymore." She had finally let everything out in the open. She had taken a stand for her freedom and, if she didn't get killed for voicing her views, at this moment, she had a feeling that things were going to change for her, at the age of sixteen.

That night, she and her sister Ivana, stayed in their room and started packing all of Jollena's clothes in a trash bag. They had a chance to do this while their mother was on the phone with one of her friends. This was it, and there was no turning back now for her. There was either going to be a severe beating when their mother thought about what Jollena said or, she was going to be kicked out on her behind, Either way, it was all in the game now.

The next day, Ann was on the warpath because, her husband had not come home all night. She was determined to mess up somebody's day, and it was not the small girls in the house. It was going to be the two she had always targeted. She suddenly remembered the conversation she had with Jollena the day before, and grabbed her by the hair, pulled her down the stairs, making sure that Jollena hit every one, on the way down to the living room.

Since you want to leave, let me show you the way to hell." She drug Jollena out the front door, in front of the neighbors, who were all doing their weekly outdoor lawn duties. She then became even more abusive by kicking Jollena in the back, stomach, and back of her head. "If you want to live on your own, let me be the first to give you what some other asshole is going to do to you." She began calling Jollena every name under the sun, and then some. The neighbors could only stand back and look in horror, as she continued to beat the crap out of her second child.

Jollena finally had a break in the beatings, and jumped up from the sidewalk, and ran as fast as her thin legs could carry her. Never once looking back to see if any of the neighbors were going to come after her. It didn't happen because everyone all but clapped. as they watched her run around the corner, and head off the street. Maybe they were cheering in their minds because, another child had escaped from the jail that their mother had made for them.

Jollena never looked back on where she rose from but kept her eye on where she was going in life. She graduated from high school, and got married to the man who had taken care of her during her struggles on the street. She had a baby girl, whom she loved very much, and who she made a promise to, that she would not raise her the same way she had been raised.

Ivana finally had a stable home for herself, and her two children to live in, along with their father. Even though she loved this man, he had a lot of issues that caused him to be very disliked by the rest of the family. He was doing the same thing to her as her father had done to her mother. She found that if she was going to make something out her life, she would have to get rid of free-loading, heavy drinking, womanizer, Roger Hayes.

"Look Roger, I'm getting very tired of putting up with your bullshit, smooth- talking, looking like a poster boy for rejects. Ivana yelled at the top of her lungs. Why don't you do us a favor and get out of my house."

"I don't have to go no damn where if I don't want to. I help pay the bills around this low-budget, filthy house. Which gives me the right to do any thing, and stay where I damn-well please." Roger yelled at her, before throwing a chair, missing and hitting the glass table instead. Ivana stood and stared at the mess he had made to something he didn't even pay for. Without a warning, she picked up a knife and drove it into his arm, cutting a half-inch gap in his wound.

She wanted to knife him again but the kids started crying. Roger ran out of the house screaming for his mother to open the door, and call the police.

Ivana knew this was going to be rough so, she called Jollena to come and pick up her kids. Later that night, she was taken into custody and booked. She stayed in the county jail for three days before Roger decided not to press charges against her. Even though she was glad to be out of jail, she swore to get back at her no- good boyfriend for having her arrested in the first place. Especially since she had two kids to raise.

Over time, she managed to get herself a job and secure a bigger place for her family, that had grown to four kids. The oldest had the job of watching the other three while she worked. Paula knew how to cook for the kids and do other things to take care of her sisters and baby brother. Ivana had raised her well to be a very responsible girl who knew how to take charge and make sure things were in order while their mother was at work.

Even though Ivana didn't live at home anymore, she would always go over to her parents home to make sure that everything was alright, and to make sure that the other two girls, who were born later on, were taken care of. The girls, Yvonne and Alisa, were being treated way better than their older sisters had been raised. If you ask me, they were being catered to with the best clothes, more freedom to go somewhere with their friends, and fed the best there was of foods.

Ivana could see that things had sort of calmed down for her mother because, she was now taking prescription drugs for whatever

49

problem she was faced with after Tanya, Jollena, and Ivana left home. One would probably say that the mother felt the girls needed to be scared to death of her, just so they would want to go and venture out on their own. It's like a mother lion sending her cubs out of the den to fetch for themselves, after torturing them to the point where the cubs would want to leave.

Mrs. Rayner was starting to do things that were out of the ordinary when it came to her medication. She started to have delusions of hearing things in the walls and the basement which would send her running around the house carrying a butcher knife and dragging her two frightened children with her. Even though the girls claimed they heard nothing she would curse at them and call them names because they didn't hear the same things she had.

Things got worse when she ended up closing herself up in her own closet in her bedroom, saying that someone was trying to kill her. She had tried to fight this illness herself by telling her doctor that she didn't feel well. He would just examine her, and give her another prescription for painkillers, water pills, and medication for her high blood pressure.

This particular day, things just wasn't going right for the girls because, they had to sit and watch their mother run around her bed, carrying a bottle of alcohol, and a half-eaten luncheon meat sandwich. They didn't know what to expect from their mother but, they were intending to find out. She was not doing the ordinary things around the house that a mother should be doing. She would just throw things and tear up her own clothes. She would open the window in her bedroom, and yell out curse words at the neighbors. After this ordeal, she would throw her clothes and underwear at anyone standing nearby her home.

The girls were so frightened that they were afraid to come out of the bathroom to see what damage their mother had done to the house and outside. After witnessing this little escapade for what seemed like hours, Alisa picked up the telephone and called the police, to come and get her mother before she hurt herself or someone else. She was scared but, if she didn't do anything about her mother, she felt that her world would fall apart right in front of her sister. What good would it do her to break down, when her mother was in such a terrible state of mind. How could she take care of things around the house, when her mom was acting like a lunatic on too much medication. The people in the neighborhood were not used to this kind of spectacle going on in their block. This was supposed to be a nice, quiet community, where a family could raise their children. Instead, they had to be confronted with the cursing and throwing of Mrs. Rayner.

As Alisa went into her parents' bedroom, she didn't know what to expect from the woman hiding in the closet. It looked like a tornado had hit that room, with the force of 3 tidal waves. Clothes were scattered all over the floor, and it smelled of alcohol and stale meat. Alisa looked all through the room for her mother, and then without warning, Mrs. Rayner popped from the closet, scaring the living daylights out of her daughter.

"BOO! She yelled at the top of her voice. You thought I was gone, didn't you? You thought I went to Mars without you, huh?"

She stared at her petrified daughter, waiting for her to respond. When the girl didn't say anything, the mother threw a whole bottle of perfume on her, and went back to the closet.

"You better get your sister and come on with me, and then you don't have to worry about nobody trying to kill you too. I got the ship ready to take off in just a few minutes." The frightened child ran to her little sister, grabbed her by the hand, and ran down the stairs just in time to see the police pull up in front of the house. She was quite embarrassed because, everyone was outside of their house talking about the chain of events that had taken place. The police asked who she was, then asked to see where her mother was.

They walked up to the second floor of the house, and began looking for Mrs. Rayner. They could not believe what they saw in the room. They just stood in the middle of the room and stared at everything out of place. One of the men started to write some notes on his pad, and looked over everything in the room as he did so. The other policeman was busy asking Alisa questions about what had taken place in the house. She told him everything she could think of that led up to her mother doing what she did to the room and, what she had done to everyone outside. This had to be the most humiliating thing that could have happen to her, at such a stage in her life.

Just as the men were finishing up their investigation, they noticed the closet door was opened a little and, they decided to see what was inside. To their horror, Mrs. Rayner was standing inside holding a loaded shotgun. They didn't want do anything too quickly that would cause her to suddenly decide to pull the trigger.

"Mrs. Rayner, will you please put the gun down and come out of the closet with your hands behind your head? We will not hurt you. We just want you to come out peacefully, so that we could talk to you about what is going on with you." One of the policemen stood a little closer to the door, and began a conversation with her.

"My name is Officer Brown, Mrs. Rayner. How are you doing? Can I get you something to drink? Is there someone you want us to call for you?" He was starting to sweat officiously, wondering what she was thinking at that moment. He also hoped that this would end without any problems arising.

"I don' t want to come out of my spaceship just yet because, I have to get it ready so that me and my kids can get out of here. Don't you know that the world is about to be crowded with aliens, and the President is one too. He is going to turn all of us into monsters and then he is going to peter pan off the planet." The story was too good to be true for these two law-enforcement agents. They had to turn their heads in order to keep from laughing in her face.

They had to keep talking to her until she decided to emerge from the closet without the gun. She was taken out of the house and placed in the squad car, with her hands in cuffs. They managed to get in touch with Ivana and Jollena, to let them know that their mother was going to the station. While Officer Brown was talking to Ivana on the phone, she started to get angry at the fact that her mother had a gun in the house that could have been fired accidentally by her.

After the mother was taken to the station for questioning, the Social worker decided that it would be best if she were taken to the mental hospital for evaluation. The ambulance was called to transport her. She fought and scratched the paramedics because, she didn't want to go on the aliens' spaceship, and be taken to the outer reaches of the planet.

Three days went by before Ivana and Jollena were able to go visit their mother. There was tension in the air, and the girls didn't know what to expect when they arrived at the hospital. Their father refused to go see his wife. He thought it would be best if he stayed out of the way until there was a white flag waving in the breeze. As far as he was concerned, she had bought this on by herself, by all the things she had done to her daughters and herself.

Even though their mother had become a patient in a mental hospital, that did not stop them from going to see her. At last, they arrived at the hospital parking lot and, there was not much to talk about until they had the chance to see what condition she was in. The girls stopped by the front desk to ask the secretary where they could find Mrs. Ann Rayner's room.

"Take the elevator up to the 6th floor, go to your left and go all the way down to the end of the hall, to the double doors. You will have to ring the bell in order for the nurse to let you enter the ward." The girls headed in the direction that was given to them and, waited for the nurse to let them into the area where their mother was housed.

Mrs. Rayner was in the television room with some of the other patients, watching a movie. When she saw the girls, a smile changed her facial expression and, she got up and walked over to her daughters as though she was ready to go with them.

"Did the both of you come to get me out of this crazy place?" She looked at them with a gleam in her eyes, as though she was a child waiting to go shopping with her mother. She headed to her room to get her things together when, a nurse on the floor called her back to the sitting room. "Mrs Rayner, you can't go in your room right now because, you have company here with you. I will let you back in after your daughters have finished visiting you, alright?" The girls watched as their mother stood there staring at the nurse as if she wanted to hit her but, decided to sit back down instead.

Jollena looked at her mother going to her seat, and turned to Ivana with a smile on her face, "Boy, talk about having control. Where was this place when we needed her to go sit down and stop using them as a punching bag". This was the first time that they actually had the chance to see someone else put their mother through the same thing she had done to them so very long ago but totally not forgotten. Ivana walked over to her mother and sat next to her. Jollena decided to sit down only after one of the male patients got up to go smoke a cigarette in the smoking room.

Ivana turned to her mother and asked, "Mama, is there anything you want us to bring to you, while you're in here?" She waited on an answer from her mother, while she was still staring at the nurse who had told her to sit back down. Even though this was like a victory dance to the girls, they really didn't like the way their mother looked in this place. Although she had put them through extreme pain and suffering, this was not looking too good for her.

Ivana decided to ask her mother one more time if she wanted them to bring her anything back from home. "Mom, is there something we can get for you at home or the store?" With that question, Mrs. Rayner jumped up and walked over to the nurses' station and started picking up things off the top of the desk, and throwing them back on the floor. Two of the male nurses came from the back of the room where they had not been seen by Ivana or Jollena, and ran up to their mother, grabbed her by the arms, and made her sit down while one of the other nurses gave her a shot in her arm. When the medication took affect, they let her go, and headed back to the area they had originally come from.

Jollena and Ivana were shocked that their mother would jump at someone else the way she did. They felt that she needed to be here because, it could have been a situation where she could have done that to someone on the street and, would have gotten hurt or killed.

There was no doubt about it, their mother was a danger to herself, and to others around her. She would have to stay here until the courts decided that she was no longer a threat to herself, and to the two children still left at home. There was going to have to be an investigation into the medications that she was taking, along with the diet pills and alcohol she would sometimes mix together. Her system was so messed up from all of the prescription drugs, that she could no longer control her actions or mood-swings. Jollena and Ivans decided it would be better if they ended their visit with their mother and let her get some rest. They promised her that they would come back the next day, at the usual time. Mrs. Rayner managed to say goodbye to her girls before her nurse helped her to her room. As they left the building, both girls decided to talk about what they were going to do to help the other two sisters at home. Both agreed that the girls would go to Ivana's for the weekend, then they would spend the rest of the week at Jollena's house because, she was off work for a couple of months, due to her injury she sustained while at work.

With their mother in the hospital, the girls did pretty well in regards to looking after their other two sisters until things got better in the home. After they had done all that they could to see that things were in order, their father decided to call his sister to come and stay at the house with him and the kids, so that Jollena and Ivana could get on with their lives of going to work and taking care of their own family.

This was a shock to them both, and they looked forward getting to the business of seeing that things got back together in their own homes. This was a good gesture for their father to do for them, since he had been having a good time going out with his friends, when he wasn't working or spinning records somewhere. With that going on, he thought enough to give them a break from the two youngest sisters.

It had been three months since their mother went into the hospital for the treatment of chemical imbalance from too many different prescriptions she had gotten from her doctor. She was doing a lot better by taking the right medication to break down the chemicals in her body. Her doctor gave her a good review in front of the judge, which was what she needed to be able to get the chance to go home to her family.

Mr. Rayner made it back home in a matter of three hours with his wife, who was in a hurry to get back to her own surroundings, and to see her daughters. She walked around the house making sure that everything was still in order when she left. Of course, she had no idea that she had totally destroyed the house when she was sick. The younger girls told her what had happened to her, and what she had done to most of her clothes.

"You mean to tell me that I did all those things to the house and to the neighbors? I actually threw all my clothes out the bedroom window, along with my underwear?" With this bit of news, she started to laugh until she had tears coming from her eyes. "I would have loved to see the expression on their faces when they got extra large size bloomers coming at them like parachutes." She got a kick out of making her neighbors' day, to brighten up the neighborhood, and to bring them out of their homes every once in a while, to see who is doing what. She made this situation a joke, while the rest of the family thought it was very tasteless and just plain rude. But, this was their mother and wife so, they couldn't just think that she would not respond to this problem like a pro.

Yvonne and Alisa were still a little frightened of their mother, and it took some time for them to realize that she was doing a lot better since leaving the hospital. Ivana and Jollena had talked to them and, had assured them that she was not going to fall back down again. It took them almost a month to realize that she was a different person this time, and hoped she would stay that way.

They finally adjusted to getting back to school, being able to see their mother before leaving in the mornings because, at first they had to depend on their sisters and aunt to take them to school. Things got back to normal in no time at all and, their father started to do his thing again. After three years had passed, things were starting to look up for Alisa because, she was going into the navy after her graduation ceremony.

She had packed all her things two weeks before graduation and, was looking forward to leaving ST.Louis to do something she always looked forward to doing, traveling. But there was something in the air that just didn't add up. One day after Jollena had taken her daughter to visit her dad and grandmother, she left for work, with the understanding that his mother would look after this precious little cargo. Somehow, little Tashina tried to follow her cousins down the backyard concrete stairs. Instead of a good evening together, this little baby had fallen down a flight of concrete stairs, and had a lump on her head the size of two half-dollars. No one even took the time to take the little girl to the hospital, which was only a couple of blocks away. They were too busy sitting around the living room drinking and listening to music.

"Grandma, Tashina fell down the backyard stairs, trying to keep up with us, said the seven year-old grandson of Mrs. Kettner." With those words, he walked the baby over to his grandmother, so that she could look at the child's forehead.

"Oh, she'll be alright, honey. She just bumped her head a little, and got a hicky, that will go away in a day or two." She put the child on the floor to take off again walking on her own, crying for her mother. This was a deliberate neglect on the part of the grandmother, who is supposed to watch over all her grandchildren as though they were precious gems. But, because of the large amount of alcohol in her system, she didn't seemed to be worried about this helpless child.

Of course she didn't want to get involved with a lot of legal work, that she felt would have taken up her whole day. She didn't really care too much for Jollena because, she thought that her son was too good to be with an eighteen year-old girl fresh out of high school. She once told Jollena, after finding out that she was going to have a baby, that she should not even bring that child into the world but, that she should get an abortion instead.

This didn't stick with Jollena because, Mrs. Kettner just wouldn't except the fact that her son (age 31) had slept with this young lady and, had decided to marry her because he didn't want her to have to go through with trying to raise a child by herself. She had tried to break them up by telling her son that Jollena was just looking for someone to take care of her for the rest of her life.

Wilson knew he had taken on a big responsibility but he loved Jollena too much to just let her take care of this child alone. Even though he knew that she could do things by herself, he decided to get a job working at an restaurant. This didn't pay too much but it did help them to take care of what they needed to survive. Things seemed to be working for them for the first couple of months after the baby was born.   They celebrated their first Christmas in their new apartment. Everyone around them could tell that they were in love and was doing a good job of taking care of their baby daughter.

But, their happiness was short-lived because they started to get on each other's nerve and, Wilson started to drink heavily. He would go next door to their neighbors' home to have a couple of drinks and listen to a drunk tell him how to treat his wife. Linda Paster and her husband Clancy had known Wilson and Jollena for only three months after they moved into their place. Linda and Jollena became good friends and spent a lot of time together. It was weird to Jollena at first because, she was not used to seeing white girls with black men, and it took her awhile to understand that Linda was just a Texas- born girl who just happen to talk as though she were black herself. Once Jollena got past this, they created a bond that was too hard for anyone to break apart.

So, it was quite hard for Linda to hear her husband tell her best friend's partner to beat up his wife, and make her do everything he said for her to do. He told Wilson to be a man and let his wife know who was boss in the house, and to keep her in her place.

"I don't believe you Clancy, how could you sit there and tell that man to beat his wife and make her act like a slave? Don't you know that slavery went out over 200 years ago? You ain't nothing but a low-down, tail-licking, dog in heat.

"Damn girl, you got some nerve talking to me like that, he yelled at the top of his voice, looking like his whole world just caved in. She had messed up his plans and he had to come up with something to say real quick or, he was going to look like a lying sack of dog mess. He jumped up out of his seat and went into the kitchen where Linda was cooking dinner and, hit her in the mouth with the back of his hand. She fell to the floor and looked up at him with such hate in her eyes. He hit her in the face again, then left the kitchen.

"Hey man, I'm getting ready to go on home because, I need to get me some dinner, Wilson said as he got up off the couch and headed for the door. I'll see you tomorrow, Clancy, man."

"Hey man, don't leave yet, don't you want to stay and help me finish the rest of this beer?" Clancy ran through the living room to the front door and grabbed Wilson by the arm. He didn't want this fool to get away because, he was having too much fun convincing another drunk to make a fool out of themselves by letting him tell them how to run their own homes and family. "I'm sorry man, that was not cool for me to do while you were here in my house. I know that I'm supposed to take care of my business when no one was here. I have to represent for all men of the world." He held out his hand so that Wilson could shake his hand. "She'll be alright man. Hell, you got to let them know that they can't just open their mouth when they haven't been spoken to yet."

Wilson shook his hand and promised to come over the next day to finish up the rest of the beer. He was too drunk to finish anything today, and he didn't want to spoil his dinner by drinking all night long. No one could out-drink Clancy when it came to polishing off some booze. The man was just a walking liquor store and, no one has beat him yet in being the champion in drinking. Even though he had a good job working at the Ford Motor Company, half of his money was spent on liquor and gambling.

Wilson opened the door and saw his wife cooking dinner and playing with the baby, he stood for a minute just looking at the two of them smiling and playing together. He had taken on a big responsibility and had to play it out just right in order for things to work for him as both a husband and a father to his little girl. "How is my little pumpkin doing? He asked as he picked his baby girl up and held her close to him. Come and go with daddy while mama is cooking."

"Wilson, I think she needs her diaper changed." Jollena said smiling at her husband and turning to go back in the kitchen to finish the evening meal. She wanted him to have a part in doing things for their child, and not wait for her to do everything herself. She wanted him to feel like a part of his child's life, as he was a part of hers.

Jollena knew that he had some problems when she met him over a year ago. There was also trouble in her life as well so, they were a perfect match for each other. She needed to escape from her abusive home and, he needed to get out from under his mother's apron strings. She often wondered to herself what she saw in this older man. She was looking for someone who was not immature and insecure about himself, so she figured things would work out with this man, who had, so far, made her life more easy. He may not have seemed like much to some, but he was a good provider, and a great father to their child.

Jollena finished cooking and, they sat down to a meal that she didn't think she could do by herself but, with some of the knowledge she received from her mother, and what she picked up from Linda, she was starting to become the perfect cook. Not bad for an eighteen year old wife and mother. After dinner was over, Jollena did the task of cleaning the kitchen and mopping the floor before going to take care of getting Tashina ready for bed. It had been a long day and, she looked forward to relaxing for the rest of the night with Wilson.

They had a good time watching horror movies that night and decided to end the night by talking about things that had taken place during the day. Jollena asked how things were going for their friends next door, and Wilson didn't seem to want to answer her.

"Wilson, you not going to tell me how my friends are doing? What, is something wrong with them or the girls?" She asked in a voice that seemed to frighten Wilson a little.

"Baby, they are alright. Why don't you just let things along and don't worry about what is going on in their marriage." He didn't mean to let that part of the conversation out of his mouth. He hoped she didn't hear what he said but he knew better than to think that about his wife because, she was good at listening to what he had to say. Therefore, the statement only made her ask another unwelcome question. "What do you mean by saying such a thing like that about their marriage? What's wrong with their marriage, Wilson? You mind as well tell me because, I'll find out anyway from Linda." She turned and looked him in the face, waiting for him to tell her what was wrong with Linda and Clancy.

Wilson turned to his wife and looked her in the eye before letting her in on the secret. "They had a fight while I was over there earlier today. Linda made a statement about something he said, which made her so mad that she called him out of his name. Clancy got mad and hit her in the face, knocking her to the floor."

"Why would he just up and hit her like that? What were you and Clancy talking about that would cause my friend to get her butt kicked by her husband?" Jollena had gotten really upset by this time and, stood up in the middle of the floor with her hands on her hips. She knew that Clancy had a bad drinking problem that had caused him to get in trouble before but, this was something a little more serious to her. Clancy was a dog in every way and everyone tried to avoid him at all cost because, he had the tendency to get other people in trouble for something that he himself had started. So Jollena knew it had to be something that involved her husband and she was going to find out what it was he said.

"Jollena, don't get in the middle of their problems, Okay? I don't want Clancy coming over here getting in my face because you were butting in their affairs, which didn't have anything to do with us."

"That's a load of bull and you know it, Wilson. Clancy is a dog and a drunk, which makes me wonder what he said that pushed Linda to speak up. You know as well as I do that Clancy has a bad habit of getting involved in other peoples' lives by starting trouble in their family, then sitting down in his own house laughing about what he had done to them. He always thought that stuff was funny but, a lot of people hate him for getting in their business so, don't you sit there on that bed and tell me to stay out of their marriage when, in fact he is the one who needs to stay out of—" She had just figured out what was going on with this story. "He told you to do something that has to do with us, didn't he?" She stood over her husband who, looked like he had just swallowed a mouse, and it got stuck in his throat.

"Okay, he told me to hit you every now and then to make you understand who was boss in our house. He also told me to make you my slave so that you would know that I am the master." He looked up at his wife with such regret in his eyes that she could do nothing but walk away from him crying to herself. He ran after her and put his arms around her tight, hoping she would not blame him for the stupid things that someone else had done.

"How could you let him put such nasty thoughts in your head? Did you plan on going along with this stupid stuff he said? Did you let him say all that stuff just to be in good with him, so you would have some one to drink with? You are as bad as he is, for letting him tell you what to do with your own wife, to destroy our marriage, and to tear down everything we have built up."

"I didn't have anything to do with what he was talking about, Jollena. I just sat on the couch and listened to what he had to say about stuff he does to his lady."

"You didn't have to let it go as far as you did, Wilson. To be honest with you, you had a lot to do with Linda getting jumped on because, you could have told Clancy to stop saying such things and change the subject. As soon as he started that foolish nonsense, you could have told him goodbye and bought your narrow behind back over here where you live.

"How can you tell a man who specializes in humiliating other people what to do in his own backyard? You know Clancy is an idiot and a liar."

"I still don't understand what made you participate in such a heinous act of sabotage, Wilson. You should try and leave alcohol along if it affects your judgement in deciding on our marriage." Jollena had said enough for the night. She would talk to Linda tomorrow, and let her know that she was sorry for what had happened to her. The both of them would have to get together and figure out what to do about Clancy. He had to be stopped before he destroys someone else's life.

The next day, Jollena got up, took a shower, and fed the baby her cereal for breakfast. She was still thinking about what had happened to Linda the night before. She wanted to tell her friend that she was there for her if she needed her. She put a roast in the oven grabbed Tashina, her bottle, and headed over to Linda's house. When she opened the door, Jollena could see her eye was swollen and red. The whole side of her face was also bruised and swollen. Jollena wanted to cry when she saw how her friend's face resembled a boxer's battered face after he lost a match.

"Oh Linda, I am so sorry about what happened to you. I didn't know what had taken place until Wilson told me late last night. I was so mad at him, I wanted to slap him in the face. He could have come home instead of letting things go as far as they did. I don't like it when he drinks because, he doesn't have the sense to limit the amount he consumes. I wish he would stop trying to be like someone he isn't." She said as she put the baby in her little baby seat.

"I don't think he had anything to do with what took place last night. He was really quiet and just sat on the couch listening to that idiot talking about what should be done to you to make you do what he wants you to do." Linda wiped her hands, which was full of egg batter, on her apron and gave Jollena a cup to get some coffee.

"I still don't think it was right for him to be a part of something that was totally tasteless and full of bull. I wish we could do something about his macho, woman-beating, drunk self. The man is too wrapped up in himself, and thinks he's jack of all trades, when in reality, he's just a master of none." They both laughed at the thought of him being master of anything except Wilson, who seems to let anybody tell him what to do with his life.

"You know what Jollena? We have a bond that is strong and we will prevail one day. We will both be doing a lot better than we are right now. You just wait and see what I'm talking about. Things will be different for the kids, and us as well. We will hold our heads up high and walk with the best of them, You'll see." Linda winked at Jollena as she continued to fix French toast for her two daughters, Tiffany and Casey. These two kids (Tiffany was three, and Casey was one) were her pride and joy and, she would do anything to protect them from him. As the months went by, things got back to normal in both apartments because. the girls made sure to keep the men from getting back together and drinking. Clancy had to do his drinking by himself, and Wilson just didn't do too much as long as he had to do it by himself, without an audience. As long as both of them were sober, they were a joy to be around, as far as the two couples getting together for dinner.

Life was great and the girls continued to be close friends, helping each other with issues they had to work out. And that didn't stop them from being close like sisters. Linda was there when Jollena went through her emotions that still haunted her. She had never gotten any help to deal with the feelings she felt from being abused as a child. She still needed counseling but, couldn't afford to pay for it. Deep inside, she was hurting and there was nothing she could physically do about it. Jollena had escaped the beatings of her mother but, the scars and emotions were still there and she had to deal with things as they were. As a child, Jollena thought that if she could be the quiet one, and just pretend that she was a part of the walls, she would be alright and able to survive the countless beatings her mother bestowed upon them. Now that she was a wife and mother herself, she still felt like there was no way she could be happy, coming from a dysfunctional home. Somehow, she had a feeling that her marriage was not going to last. But, for right now, she would pretend to be normal and happy, never once taking the time to piece together complex problems that would show that her patterns learned in childhood, had followed her into adulthood, and is the reason for the feelings she harbors in her life.

She always felt that she had married the wrong man, although he's busy going his own way. She was just fortunate enough to find him when she was beginning to understand what was going on in her life, and what she intended to do with it since leaving home. She didn't feel like she was ready to be anybody's wife, but she wanted to try to have a normal life the way she had seen in some of her high school friends' parents. Unfortunately, that was not going to happen in this marriage.

Clancy had succeeded in getting Wilson to be the master he thought he should be. He started to drink a lot more when Clancy was around, and they both would take off and go out for most of the night. This was the last straw for Jollena, and nothing was going to keep her from getting revenge on Wilson for the way he had treated her. She sat up late one night waiting for his return home. He finally showed up at three a.m. with his breath smelling like three liquor factories.

"Where have you been all night, Wilson? Did you think to phone and let me know if you were alright or not? The next time, let me know if you're going to be coming home right before the birds wake up, Okay?

"You didn't have to wait up for me, baby I was coming home earlier but, Clancy was the one doing the driving so, you know I had to go where he went." Wilson blurted out in a loud voice, not realizing that he was talking too loud. The baby started to cry and. Jollena gave her a bottle to put her back to sleep.

"Baby, I'm sorry and, I promise to be home at a earlier time when we go out again.

I'll tell Clancy to drop me off when he wants to go somewhere else. At those last words, he toppled over in bed and fell asleep before she could say anything else to him.

Three days later, while Jollena was cooking dinner for her family, Wilson was drinking next door again with the neighborhood, two-legged hound dog. There was a loud noise from the apartment they were in. She grabbed her child, and ran to the door, banging as loud as she could. Linda came to the door crying and holding both her children.

"What is all the noise over here about? She screamed and looked at Linda in complete terror.

"Clancy was playing with his gun and accidentally fired a shot into the wall, right above the childrens' bed. He was trying to show your husband how to shoot at you, without killing you." With that, Jollena ran pass Linda and pulled her husband up out of the chair he sat in and told him to come home. Clancy looked at Wilson with an evil eye, and turned up his bottle of booze to his lips without even saying a word of being sorry for what he did.

"I don't want to go home right now, so get your damn hands off me. I will come home when I get good and ready, Miss Jollena. I don't need no teenager to tell me when to come home." Linda couldn't take what she was hearing any longer and, grabbed Wilson by the arm, and pulled him in the kitchen in order to talk to him.

"Look man, that teenager is now your wife. The both of you have been married for seven months now. You didn't think she was a teenager when you laid down with her, or when you put that ring on her finger and said you will love her till death do you part."

"That is still a teenager and you know it. I should have listened to my mother. She told me not to get mixed up with her or any of her family."

"What has got you so wired up today, Wilson? Did Clancy say something to you when I went in the bathroom? You need to tell me what is going on with you and my husband. I need to know if he is doing or saying something bad about your wife. You need to sober up and realize that if you don't stop this stupid charade you are playing, you will lose both your wife and your child. And by the way, don't let Clancy tell you anything about anyone around here because, he is skating on thin ice tonight.

Wilson looked her in the face and cried like a baby. I was told by your husband that Jollena was seeing some man while I was at work. He said one day, he saw her leave the house and get into a car with this man, with my child in the back seat.

"Tell me one thing Wilson, what was he doing that he saw this take place because, he was supposed to be at work. He was not here so, where could he have possibly saw her? Linda stood up, and put the kids back to bed. She then went into the living room where Jollena and Clancy were sitting, fusing at one another. She asked Jollena to go and talk to her husband, while she had a conversation with Clancy.

When it was all over, Jollena and Wilson went home and he fell right to sleep on the couch. Jollena put her baby to bed, and put on her nightclothes. She took a last look at this man whom she didn't know anymore, and wondered why he would let one man ruin his marriage.

It just didn't seem like something a real man would do to his family. This seemed like the stupid actions of an idiot, who loves to play the part of a donkey's behind.

The next two days were bitter for Jollena because, she had not talked to her husband since he said what he did in front of her and her best friend, who happen to have a husband who enjoys making other people's life a living nightmare. He, on the other hand, didn't like the idea of his wife not saying a word to him. The silence in the air only made him more mad at her and, he decided to do something about it. He walked into the kitchen where she was fixing herself and her child some breakfast when, he started in on her with the things that Clancy had said took place while he was at work. Jollena did not care to hear any of this garbage anymore so, she went into the living room and turned on the t.v.

"I want to know is any of what Clancy said true or not? He waited on an answer to come from his wife which, none came his way. He grabbed her by the arm, lifted her up off the couch, and asked her the same question again. "Jollena, will you please answer my question. I want to know if you have been unfaithful to me while I was at work?"

Jollena had enough of this interrogation and pulled her arm away from him. "If you want to believe your friend next door, then you go right ahead and have yourselves a good time at my expense. I am getting tired of you and, I am totally getting tired of your drunken friend getting in our business. So, if you want someone to talk to, go on over to his house, the both of you jump in his car, and go screw yourselves." She pushed pass him and went into the bathroom to get away for a minute.

Three months later, Wilson had moved out of the house because, there was no use in causing his wife anymore grief than she had gone through already. He promised to keep giving her money every week to take care of the rent and other things she needed to care for her baby and herself. Life was starting to look up for her now. Linda had once told her so when they first met, after Jollena moved in. She could finally be her own boss, in her own house. She didn't have to answer to anybody but herself and her child. No more abuse for her. She had succeeded in what she always wanted, to live a life without beatings, screaming, and the chance to see her other man, without having to sneak around with him any more. He had been her knight in shining armor, and she was his princess. And they were happy for the rest of the time that they lived in that apartment.

A year later in the summer of 1979, they were living in their new place and, Jollena had gotten a job as a waitress in a large restaurant, and her new boyfriend, Reginald, was working at a hotel in the county, at night. They were doing fine until the day Jollena took her child over to her ex-husbands' mom's house. After going to the hospital to see if her daughter had a serious head injury, the two of them made it back home okay. The doctor said Tashina would be fine. She had only gotten a minor injury to her forehead, and only needed to be watched overnight. Jollena decided to stay home with her child for a week, in order to make sure she was doing great. She had planned to stay home for the labor day weekend, when her supervisor told her she would be fired if she didn't return to work the next day.

Not wanting to leave her child because, she was concerned about her, Reginald talked Jollena into going work. He reassured her that everything would be fine. She was nervous at work that morning, for some strange reason. She kept having a hard time listening to her supervisor tell them what the menu was for that day. Fifteen minutes after the restaurant opened for business, she got a call from the hospital, telling her that her child was in the emergency room in intensive care. Jollena dropped the phone and headed for the kitchen area. She didn't know what had happened after that because, she had passed out in the kitchen, and was taken to the women's locker room by two of the chefs. When she came around, they were telling her that her friend was waiting on her downstairs in the employees entrance to the building.

"Will someone help her downstairs, and make sure that she gets in the car safely? I don't want anything to happen to her. She has been through enough already." Her supervisor said with such hurt in her voice. She felt guilty about telling Jollena to come to work, knowing that her child had been sick. She wished that she could have taken back what she said when Jollena tried to take off one more day. Everyone in the restaurant was hoping that little Tashina would pull through. They all said a prayer for the little girl and her mother, in the kitchen, before going to their stations.

As soon as Jollena got to the hospital, the nurses took her into a waiting room and, said that a doctor would be with her as soon as possible. It seemed like hours for Jollena because no one seemed to want to tell her anything. But, she waited patiently until a doctor finally appeared in the room. She introduced herelf as the doctor who had taken care of Tashina when she came in.

"Miss Rayner, I have some bad news for you. We tried to do everything possible to save your baby, but there was nothing we could do. She was without oxygen a little too long. Her body just gave out and she passed on. Jollena felt sharp pains in the pit of her stomach and fell to the floor screaming and kicking for her child. Reginald had to hold on to her because, she was not in her right state of mind. The doctor wanted to calm her down but, Jollena would not let this woman give her a shot. She tried to knock the needle out of the doctor's hand with her foot. Jollena had a fear of needles, and would fight anyone trying to to give her a shot with one. She had it in her mind that the hospital was trying to kill her, and she refused to let them have the last say.

Reginald asked the doctor if she would give her a pill instead of the needle, to calm her down before they would talk to her again. Two minutes later, a nurse came into the room with a pill and a cup of water for Jollena to take. The room was cleared out until the medicine had taken affect on her, then the doctor returned to get her to sign some papers releasing her child to the medical examiner.

Jollena was led into a room down the hall from where she was at, and she stood in the middle of the floor and looked at the little bundle laying on the table, wrapped in a blanket. Reginald walked her over to the table, and put a chair near so that Jollena could sit closer to her child. At first, she was too afraid to pick up the bundle because, she thought that she might drop the baby because the medicine had her a little dizzy. But, finally, she let Reginald put the baby in her arms, so she could hold and kiss her child one more time. Once Jollena was holding her, she did not want to let her go. She held her close to her face, and heard the last bit of air in her body leave her.

After leaving the hospital, Jollena and Reginald went over to her parents' house, where the other sisters were waiting for her to come over. They had no idea what they were going to say to their sister, concerning the death of her only child but, they knew that they had to be there to show their support. After all, no one had gone through anything like this and therefore, had no idea what Jollena was feeling at this point.

The house was still as Jollena walked around from room-to-room looking at the other kids playing with toys they had bought with them. She stared at them for what seemed like hours, at the same time, wanting to die herself. She thought it had been her fault that her child was gone because she had left her alone, with the one person that was supposed to have taken care of her, her grandmother. Thinking of this only caused her to start to cry uncontrollable. Everyone ran to her in order to let her know that she was not in this world alone, that they were going to be with her through all this.

As they were helping her to sit down, her mother jumped up from her seat and yelled at Jollena. "Girl, you need to shut up all that noise and get on with your life. It's not like you can't have anymore kids." These words cut through Jollena like a knife. How could her mother be so cold-hearted to her? How could she let something like that, come out of her mouth after her daughter had lost her only child. The other girls just stared at their mother in sure horror, wondering what had come over her, and how could she just pretend that this was no big deal. Of course she had learned to do this real well throughout her life because, she really didn't care too much for her own kids, let long their children.

She had no feelings for her children at the time of the abuse she inflicted upon them so, this was no surprise to the girls when they heard her say what she did to Jollena, who turned to her mother with hate in her eyes, and let her know exactly how she felt about that statement.

"Mama, you have all of us, Ivana had her four kids, and Tanya has her two. The only one I had in this world is gone. You don't understand what it feels like to have your only child die, and you have to be the one to bury her. So don't tell me nothing about stopping my crying because, as long as I live, I'm going to cry for the child I lost." And with those words, Jollena ran upstairs to the bathroom and locked the door. All she wanted was to cry by herself, with no one to mess with her. But, that didn't last too long because, Tanya ran up the stairs and started banging on the bathroom door for Jollena to open it.

Jollena, open this door now, dear. Come on, let me in so that I can make sure you're okay." She continued to knock until Jollena finally opened the door. All her sisters were standing outside of the bathroom, waiting to see her when she did come out.

"I just wanted to make sure you were not trying to end your life as well." Tanya said, in a calm voice so as not to scare her. "We are just concerned about you being left alone by yourself right now so, where you go, we will go as well." This kind of made Jollena smile for just a moment because, she had just gotten a mental picture of her sisters following her around the house from room to bathroom, making sure she didn't try to take her life. Even though they were there with her, she still felt like she had to go through this by herself.

While the girls were upstairs with Jollena, their mother was busy on the phone calling over to the child's other grandmother's house to invite them to come over.

The atmosphere in the house was not a good one for both families, who had gathered together to mourn the lost of Jollena and her ex-husbands' child. There was bad blood between these two parents and no one could change that, no matter how many times they all got together. Jollena blamed his mother for the lost of her child and would never forgive her for not taking her daughter to the hospital when she first fell.

Everyone was busy talking about little Tashina and other things in their lives. When out of the blue, Wilson walked over to Jollena and sat down beside her. He wanted to talk to her in order to get things out in the open but she didn't seem to notice that he was sitting there.

"I want to talk to you, Jollena, if you don't mind me sitting here beside you. I just feel like we should put our differences aside and just deal with the present situation." Jollena turned toward him with hatred in her tear-filled eyes and, hit him so hard, that he would wind up in the same place as her child now lay.

"I don't have anything to say to you, Wilson. As a matter of fact, I didn't even ask for you to come to my parents' house. Things will never be the same for the both of us. I have lost the only thing that I really cared about in this world." She turned her head away from Wilson, and looked into space.

"Oh, you think you are the only one here who lost something? I lost a child too, you know. She was my only child, as well as yours. We both lost out on something precious."

"If she was so precious to you, why did you not take her to the hospital when she fell down those stairs, huh? You tell me why you just sat there with your family, while your child was crying and hurt? You come up with an answer for those questions, and I'll be more than glad to be in your corner. But until then, stay the hell out of my face, with all of your so-called caring."

"Jollena, please don't feel like that towards me. It was my fault, I know this, and I was not in my right mind at the time that she fell. I have to deal with this for the rest of my life. All I ask is that you forgive me, and let's just be friends." He grabbed her by the hand but, she just pulled away from him. "Okay, I see we are not going to get to settle this today but, I am not going to give up on you, Jollena. If you need my help with the funeral, let me know what it cost and I will give you the money."

"Let me make this clear so that you can understand. I don't need anything from you, nor will I ever except anything from you. As far as my child's funeral is concerned, I will take care of it myself, thank you. I don't need your money, Wilson." After this blow to the head, he took the hint, and got up from the couch. He had lost his wife and child forever. He was never going to get over this day, and he would always remember the words that took place between the two of them.

It had been a long day and, everyone was starting to get tired so, Wilson and his family said their good-byes, and said they would see everyone the next day for the funeral. After they had gone, Jollena was ready to leave also because, she was too exhausted to do anything else for the rest of the day. She asked Reginald to take her home, so that she could get some sleep. She told her sisters and parents that she would see them later. Behind today, the only thing she wanted to do was lay down and cry herself to sleep.

After the funeral, everyone went back to Jollenas' parents' home and had something to eat. The conversation centered around how much of a fool Wilson's family acted because they were not allowed to ride in the limousine with Jollena and her family. They felt that Wilson and his mother should have been in the car with Jollena because, they were family. But, because they didn't get to ride, they decided to do one tasteless act to finish off the day. They waited until after the preacher had concluded the graveside service before taking almost all of the flowers that were sitting on the site, and transferring them to their car.

Jollena had a chance to see what was going on as she was being led back to the limo. What she saw was rude and totally disrespectful to her child's grave. They were putting large pots of flower arrangements from her job, and another one that She and Reginald had bought, with a large pink ribbon attached, with the words "TO OUR DARLING BABY", which was layered in 14k gold letters. This was supposed to have stayed at the grave sight but, they decided to take it for themselves as if they had paid for it. This last act of foolishness was all that Jollena could take. She burst out in tears, as she got into the car and they drove off. She was never going to forgive Wilson for this rude act upon her child. He was going to pay for everything that they had done because, she felt he could have told them not to dishonor him.

As time passed, Jollena was able to put her life back in order and start to do the things she really wanted to do in her life. She and Reginald were married in August 1983, after a long relationship that lasted for four years. She was later blessed with two children, a girl and a boy, who were ten years apart. This marriage was going to last no matter what she had to go through. She had made a vow to herself that she was not going to get married a third time, so this one had to go well, and it did last for eighteen years.

The girls all had gotten older and a lot wiser with their problems and successes in life. Jollena was happy with her family and business that she and her husband owned, Ivana was a successful marketing advisor, and had five grand children. Yvonne had one child and, was a financial consultant for a large stock exchange, and Alisa was married with one child, and was successful in the armed forces, which she escaped to in order to get away from the problems she faced living at home with her mother.

The girls were very close in that they always tried to do things together as a family. A couple of times, they all met at Alisa's house for a sleepover. The evening went well with the girls going out on the town, then going back to the house to continue their party. They sat up all night talking about the things that took place in their parents' house. They talked about the abuse that was thrown upon them early in their childhood.

Ivana remembered that one faithful day that her mother came home unexpectedly and found out that she had left out the house to go to a party. She was thrown down the stairs by her mother, her clothes were torn off her, and she was beaten with the handle of a rake for what seemed like hours before she was forced to let the child go because, she had beaten her till she was knocked out cold. There was blood all over the floor because, she had hit Ivana several times in the head. Her arms were cut in several places, from her elbows to the wrists. One of her legs were so swollen that she would have had to stay off of it for several months, had she gone to a doctor but, Mrs. Rayner took care of the problem herself because she didn't want the child services to find out anything.

Jollena recalled the time when she was beaten for several hours because her mother thought that she had taken a large amount of money from her purse. She dragged Jollena down to the basement, took an extension cord, and started to beat her from the head, down to her legs. She even took her own legs and wrapped them around Jollena's head, so that the girl couldn't hardly breath. The beatings lasted for almost an hour before Mrs. Rayner decided to stop because she was too tired to continue. She tried to make Jollena tell that she had took the money but, Jollena was not about to lie and say that she did such a thing, when she knew that she had not done what her mother accused her of.

Jollena still had those same bruises and marks on her body, even though she was now an adult, with a family of her own. Alisia and Yvonne sat in amazement at what their sisters were telling them. They had managed to escape the wrath of their mother because they were not yet born. They only remembered the trouble they had with her as she went through the motions of being in and out of the hospital for mental depression, caused by whatever that had occurred later in her life.

Even though most of their lives were filled with pain and abuse, both verbally and physically, the girls were determined to stick together and help each other if they felt that one of them were about to do the same thing as their mother had done. They felt that the abuse had to stop somewhere and, it had to end with them all working together as a team.

They knew they would have to rely on each other because, they had never gone to see a therapist about the trauma that they had undergone by being told they were nothing but dumb and stupid, and would never amount to anything in life. They had never gotten any warm hugs from their mother so, when they had kids of their own, they found it hard to show their children how much they cared for them. This was a task that they had to learn on their own, without anyone being there to show them how to be affectionate to their children.

"By us getting together like this, we have a chance to see what each person is carrying around with them through life." Said Yvonne as she reached over and hugged Ivana and Jollena. She never had an idea just how much hurt and despair each of her sisters were toting around with them, even though they were successful women, with a family to raise.

"No wonder you guys were always trying to do harm to yourselves, you didn't know what to do to get rid of the pain." Alisa said, with a sad look on her face. She wished she had tried a little harder to get her sisters to cope with the anguish and violence that they carried with them no matter how they tried to hide.

As far as they were concerned, hiding played a major part in their survival. They tried very hard to hide the pain by pretending it just was a part of growing up, and they were never supposed to talk to anyone about what took place in the home. But, there were a lot of good times when their mother was out with her friends. They had a chance to talk about how they were going to treat their kids when they finally had some of their own. They talked about how they were going to have a better life than the one that was thrust upon them by their mother. And with God on their side, that is exactly what they set out to accomplish, and to prove to their mother, that they were not dumb and stupid.

One time, while their mother and father were gone for the evening, they wanted to give their parents something for their anniversary, by giving a party and charging admission. They had fun planning this party because they had bought a lot of supplies with their own money and, they had everything set when the time came. Jollena laughed out loud at the thought of talking about this particular event because they had to pick up their mom's stereo/bar, and take it down in the basement in order to have some music to play.

"Do you remember how much trouble we had, and almost dropped the thing down the stairs, trying to hold on to it for dear life?" Ivana asked, laughing just as hard as Jollena did.

"Yeah, and do you remember how we thought we were going to have to play records on the thing from the angle that it sat in, up against the wall, stuck?" Said Jollena, as they raised their glasses and made a toast to the occasion.

"I was too young to remember what you guys did that night. But, I do recall the problem you had with getting it back up the stairs at the end", Smiled Yvonne, as she raised her glass to toast with her sisters. She was really the lucky one in the bunch, not to have gone through what seemed like a convent to the other girls. Having to be put in that situation was not good for any child, let alone three at once, being treated in the same exact way.

"Hey guys, do any of you remember the time mama left to go out and we decided to go outside on the front porch, and Sandy locked the door behind her, as she ran out to be with us?" She thought ghosts were after her."

"I remember that quite well, said Jollena, as she turned to Ivana, and started to laugh. I remember someone here had to go next door to borrow a ladder in order for us to get back in the house. Ivana looked at everyone and, laughed out loud. "I had to go and get the ladder, because if we had not gotten back inside the house, mama would have come home and beat the rest of the skin off our bodies. You guys don't know how scared I was.

I know Ivana, and I know that we had a hard time getting you inside the second floor window, in order to answer the telephone because, she was calling to check on us. Now, do you all remember that little problem?"

"You know what, we have been through a lot and, have done a lot too." Said Ivana, with a little sadness in her face. We had to do something in order to escape the abuse and mental problems we encountered. It was like being in a fantasy or something."

"Yeah, but it was such a painful fantasy when she found out what we had done," said Jollena as she smiled and grabbed her sister by the arm and hugged her. This was a sign for the other girls to join to and embrace each other and, to thank each other for being there while they went through the hardest part of their lives. They had been lucky enough to be in the same category with a few of the ones who managed to survive being put in numerous foster homes and then sent back to the same environment where the abuse took place. Three out of five girls were put through a lot of pain and suffering in order for one person to be satisfied that she had ruined their chances of ever being the mothers they had hoped to be because, they would always be fighting with themselves trying to keep from becoming the same abusive mother that they had run away from.

They had to depend on their own instincts and emotions to learn the difference between what was abuse and what were spankings. This was hard for them, considering the fact that they had not gotten any help from social workers or any other services that were available to children of abusive parents. They had done it by themselves, only depending on each other for support. In their eyes, this was all they needed because, no one else would understand what they were, or had gone through.

It was 1995, and the women had taken on new attitudes and perspectives in their everyday lives. They no longer felt threaten by their mother, and they were getting on with what was more important now. They had the task of taking care of their parents, who had gotten old, and couldn't get around anymore like they used to in their younger years. Mr. Rayner had been in the hospital twice, for heart surgery. Mrs. Rayner couldn't get out too much either because she had been having trouble with her legs swelling up on her.

The house needed a lot of work done on it so, all the daughters got together and decided on what to do in regards to decorating and painting. They never guessed that they would have to redo the house that they hated so much when they were kids. But, this was going to be easy for them to accomplished because they now had a lot of help, they had men in their lives who could do most of the work that needed to be done.

It took them at least a year to do everything that needed to be done in and outside the home. The neighbors couldn't believe what the girls had done for their parents. They watched these kids grow into young ladies, who now showed they loved their parents by fixing up the home that they intended to live the rest of their days in.

This was a love that no one but the girls could understand and, this was a way of healing for them. No one had to tell them that if they just kept on believing in themselves, they could overcome anything that was put before them. They would learn that keeping anger hidden inside was no way to deal with emotions and pinned up depression. The lord had bought them a long way from where they had come from and, it would be the lord who would watch over them as they all go through trials and tribulations for whatever time they have left with their parents. They all had gone through a lot during the time between fixing the house and raising their own kids. Ivana had been suffering from depression and bad headaches. Her pain had gotten so bad that, she tried to commit suicide a couple of times and had to be admitted to the hospital for a few months.

Her kids were taken care of by the other sisters until she was able to be released from the doctor's care. Once she was treated for both problems, she soon regained her life and started back to work. Jollena went through a few problems of her own which caused her to have considerable amounts of pain to her back due to the job injury she had gotten. She had trouble walking without the use of a cane, and was not able to stand up to do anything around the house because, the pain was so bad that she would have to lay down on her side and not move.

Jeanette Williams

Her doctor put her on a lot of pain medication and, she had to go through a lot of physical therapy to regain the use of her legs, and start to move around the house. It got bad for her during the holiday season because, she had been used to working and taking charge of the things that needed to be done for the kids. Her husband Reginald had been doing a lot to cover the household without her and, she was starting to feel as though she was not needed in the home anymore. She tried to get disability but the system said that she was not disabled enough to get compensation every month. But, this didn't stop her from trying once more, only to be rejected for the second time. At Christmas time, she was starting to get depressed and had no where else to turn so, she came up with the solution to leave her family so that they would not have to worry about her and, she would not be a burden to them. She sat her 4-year-old son in front of the t.v. and went into the bedroom to take a handful of pain pills. She felt that this was the only way to end her pain. Just when she was about to take them in her mouth, the lord sent a message to her by having the phone ring and Jollena answered it. Reginald had called to talk to her while he was on his lunch break. She started crying on the phone when she heard his voice.

"What is wrong with you Jollena? Why are you doing all that crying on the phone?" He waited while she got herself together and, told him how she couldn't take the pain anymore and wanted to end her own life. Upon hearing this, he yelled to his supervisor, to get permission to keep talking to his wife, in order to keep her from killing herself.

It took him an hour to convince Jollena that killing herself would only cause the family more pain then she was going through right now. He let her know that God didn't want her to take away something that didn't belong to her in the first place. He had a way of bringing her back to reality because, he was a born-again Christian.

Things were not always great for the both of them because, they had, at one time, been strong users of drugs, which almost killed the both of them. They were strung out on cocaine, speed, uppers and downers, and they were heavy smokers of pot, mixed with LSD. Jollena finally had to stop because, she was having pains in her chest. Reginald stopped sharp one day when he almost had a heart attack. They both joined a church in the neighborhood one Easter and never went back down that road again.

That was 10 years ago and they were determined to keep their children from making the same mistake they did. It stands to reason why Reginald would be fighting so much to keep his wife from ending her life. He considered her life to be a blessing from God, and she had to understand that only he could take her out of this world.

Jollena finished talking to her husband, then went to see about her son, whom she had not realized, was still sitting in the living room, watching cartoons. She grabbed him and held him close, all the time thinking about what a mistake she almost made by wanting to end her life. She looked around the room and started feeling better about herself for resisting the temptation to leave all what she had accomplished, behind her. She suddenly remembered her childhood, and how she had seen one of her foster parents being buried and, made the promise to herself to cling to life, and be thankful for every breath she took. Even though she still suffered from back pain, she learned to deal with it and, depend on the lord to help her when she had trouble. Tanya had come home again, with her two children, to start her life all over. She had gone through a lot of trouble in her everyday life, and she was trying to put her life back together after taking drugs, prostitution, and stealing from department stores, in order to get money to feed her children. She once tried to commit suicide, by putting a gun to her own head and pulling the trigger but, no bullets were in the chamber. With depression setting in, she decided to go back home where her sisters would be able to help her, as well as themselves. They all needed each other at this point.

Yvonne was busy working and traveling to different cities in between taking care of her son. She was having too much fun to really pay attention to what was going on with the others, since she was the baby of the girls. She never had to contend herself with worrying about what had happened to three of her sisters because, at the time, she was not yet born. This gave her the upper hand when it came to being abused by her mother. She had escaped the continued beatings, hitting, and the loads of verbal and mental abuse.

Her years at home were filled with love and constant understanding, and she was able to go out on dates, something that was totally not allowed when the other girls were growing up. But, even though she had all that freedom, she still ended up moving out of the home, and moving in with her boyfriend's parents. They were very kind people, and took her in as though she were one of their relatives. She still had to get up every morning and go to school. She even had a job working in their restaurant, as a cashier. This continued until she graduated from high school, then she got a job working for a big company.

Alisa had to go through a lot while living at home because, she had to watch her mother go through mental problems. She had to take on the stress of doing the cooking and cleaning, and shopping for food, after she got out of class at the end of the day. It was putting a lot of stress on her to finish high school. But, she managed to graduate and, decided to go into the army in order to get away from all the problems of home.

She did what she had to do get away from her mother and, her constantly absent dad. Once she had gotten away, she started to feel like she had something to live for. She would be able to put the past behind her and make a career in the army. When she came home on leave, she was able to enjoy the time she spent with her family. She had only wanted to stay in the army for two years but, once she finished her training and got promoted, she decided to stay a little longer. She got married to a wonderful man who, took a lot of time with the family and did a lot of work on her parents' home.

They had their ups and downs just like every one else in the world but they managed to work things out. They waited a few years before having any children of their own, and it paid off because, they had the chance to get their careers in place, and bought beautiful homes. Alisa's life has always been filled with peace and tranquility. If she had any problems, she didn't show it to anyone in the family, she might have kept it to herself in order to do what the rest of the girls had tried to do, and that was to deal with whatever came her way. She is the milestone for the rest of the girls, and she tries to keep the family together. She would sometimes make jokes about her living in a dysfunctional family setting, but everyone who knew her, had the idea that she was just pulling their legs. Boy, were they ever so wrong in that statement. The girls had a way of fooling a lot of people into thinking that their home setting was made up like the Brady bunch but, it was far from that sort of glamour. Now, each one is living the way she wants to without the hassle of wanting to do harm to themselves, or having to suffer from acute depression everyday of their lives.

Even though they were constantly abused as children, not knowing if anyone was going to come and rescue them from the torture that they had to endure for so long, they managed to make it through the storm and find their way to the other side of life. They still loved their parents and, would never let them go without anything that could make them happy. They knew that it would be hard to forgive their parents for allowing the state to put them in foster homes but, they also knew that they couldn't just keep living the nightmares of their life so, the healing had to begin where the pain left off.

There are over 2.5 million children in the world who never make it back to their homes, and there are a lot of children who continue to be pushed through the system of being forgotten and alone in the world. These are the ones who need the miracle of someone to talk to and help them to adjust to the world around them, after they are taken from an abusive home. Sometimes foster homes can be a large help and, other times it could do more harm then good to a frighten child. Fortunately, the Rayner sisters were helped when they were placed in other homes. They had someone there to help them adjust and become the strong girls that they turned out to be. If they could be face-to-face with all of the people that lifted a hand and took them in, they would thank them for the chance they took by not letting more children slip through the cracks.

Jeanette Williams

When a child is being put to harm

How could we let this hurt go on?

Who's right and who's wrong?

It's time to set the story straight

Wake up now, or it will be too late.

Before we have to take the blame,

Stop the violence in the "House of Pain."

Jeanette M. Williams

ABOUT THE AUTHOR

Jeanette Williams lives in a beautiful home in St. Louis, Missouri, where she spends a lot of time writing and enjoying being with her husband and two children. She is a member of the International Women's Writing Guild. She is currently working on her second novel.

www.ingramcontent.com/pod-product-compliance
Lightning Source LLC
Chambersburg PA
CBHW030355290526
45785CB00004B/1767